COARSE FISHING FOR BEGINNERS

The
Arnewood School Prize

Awarded to

Michael Emerton

Headteacher

The Royalty Fishery, on the famous Hampshire Avon, is regarded as one of the finest coarse venues in Britain.

Coarse Fishing

FOR BEGINNERS

•

KENNETH MANSFIELD

•

NEW EDITION

•

EDITED BY

CHRIS CLIFFORD

foulsham
LONDON • NEW YORK • TORONTO • SYDNEY

foulsham

The Publishing House, Bennetts Close,
Cippenham, Berkshire, SL1 5AP, England.

ISBN 0-572-02346-4
Copyright © 1997 W. Foulsham Co Ltd

Cover photograph © *Coarse Angling* magazine.

Text photographs reproduced with kind permission of the
Angling Times.

Typeset by Grafica, Bournemouth
Printed in Great Britain by Cox & Wyman, Reading

Contents

Foreword

As a visit to a tackle shop or a few hours spent in reading the angling press will make all too clear, angling today is encumbered by a vast mass of theory, practice, specialist information and gadgetry. The basic principles tend to become obscured.

This book is an attempt to clarify those basic principles. The recommendations on tackle take advantage of all the best modern developments, and the methods described, while containing up-to-date ideas, are founded on centuries of experience.

I have made a number of definite statements to which there are countless exceptions; and I have also suggested various tackle to use. Many experienced anglers may disagree with me but my aim has been to give the beginner something definite to work on instead of a confusion of alternatives.

Although this naturally limits the scope of the book it furthers my aim, which is to bring the complete beginner to the waterside, sensibly equipped and with a reasonable chance of catching fish of various species right away.

If I do that I shall have succeeded. When the newcomer to angling has experienced a season's fishing, mastered the manipulation of rod, reel and line, and caught a few fish he may want to experiment further. There are scores of advanced books to help him.

Throughout the book I have regarded the angler as being right-handed and male.

I think the only abbreviation I have used is 'b.s.'. This stands for 'breaking strain'.

CHAPTER 1

Preliminaries

English fishing is split into two distinct categories -- coarse and game. The latter describes the pursuit of salmon and trout using lures and flies. Coarse fishing covers all other species and it is these which this book is designed to help you catch. Although salmon and trout spend the majority of their lives in fresh water they are not classed as coarse fish. It is very important to remember this as the two disciplines are governed and licensed seperately.

The species of interest to coarse anglers are barbel, bleak, bream, carp, chub, dace, eel, grayling, gudgeon, perch, pike, roach, rudd, catfish and zander. The methods needed to catch all these fish are many and varied, and hopefully, after reading this book, you will have enough knowledge and confidence to tackle them.

Coarse fishing is undoubtedly the largest participation sport in this country, and has been for many years. For anyone looking to take up the sport, remember - patience is a virtue and results may not come immediately. But once that first fish is hooked you have walked through the door of a pastime that will give a lifetime of pleasure.

Most of the species previously mentioned can be caught nearly all over the country. The most numerous will be covered in greater detail, and the least encountered will have more brief coverage. This is because some of the methods required to catch these fish are more advanced and not really suitable for the beginner.

According to their nature and their requirements coarse fish may live in weeded canals, deep pits, sluggish rivers or fast, sparkling streams, but they have one thing in common. They spawn some time during March, April, May and June.

▲ The River Wye is renowned for superb chub, barbel and roach fishing.
▼ Large rivers such as the Trent, shown here at Collingham, provide a variety of swims. This wide stretch is ideal for bream.

Small streams are often overlooked by anglers, but many of them provide first-class fishing and interesting variety. Chub will favour deep pools with plenty of cover ▲; dace will congregate in the streamy, shallower water ▼.

Close Seasons

All coarse fishing in the country is governed by the Environmental Agency. This body, split into regions, sets the rules over when and where you can fish, sets the fee for the national licence which every angler is required to buy and carries out restocking and fish study. The national licence is available from most post offices but there are other selected places such as certain shops and fisheries who can supply them. A statutory close season runs on many waters in England and Wales, from March 15 to June 15 inclusive. This is designed to give the fish a period of rest during spawning, although weather and temperature may cause this to occur outside these dates. There are however, many areas around the country which are not governed by a close season. If in doubt contact your local Environmental Agency office to check – these rules are important and there is a very hefty fine for any angler who ignores them!

Besides the national rules you may also come across angling club restrictions. Most waters are governed by some sort of angling club, from which you may have to buy either a day or season ticket to fish. Your local tackle dealer will tell you which clubs exist in your particular area. One very important fact to remember is that the movement of fish from one water to another is illegal. If you plan to do this you must gain written permission from the Environment Agency. The reason for this strict control is to stop the spread of infectious fish diseases, notably spring viraemia of carp (SVC), which is highly dangerous to many species and can wipe out whole fisheries.

Permission to Fish

The very sound of the words 'licence to fish' gives an idea of complete freedom, and the newcomer to angling with such a licence in his wallet may well think that all he has to do is to find a stretch of water and start fishing. I am afraid that is just not so.

These days it is not often necessary to write personally to the owner. Much of the country's coarse fishing water is leased to angling clubs, membership of which carries with it the right to fish the club's waters. Many clubs also issue short-period or day tickets for the convenience of anglers visiting the area.

Some owners of water (private lakes and certain pits and ponds are the usual type) issue fishing tickets through agents, usually the local fishing tackle dealer. Wherever you go the tackle dealers on the spot are able and willing to tell you where you can fish in the locality and to sell you any necessary tickets – and, of course, such items of tackle as you may need. A day's fishing is a relatively inexpensive form of relaxation.

There may be some exceptions to the rule about getting permission to fish, but merely buying a licence does not confer a right to fish in any waters. Wherever you are, it is advisable to find out the exact position before you start to fish.

The regional Environment Agency welcomes the cooperation of the angling public in reporting any evidence of pollution in their areas so that appropriate action can be taken.

How to Start

If you are a real beginner knowing nothing about the subject, I suggest you travel around your locality, ask questions of tackle dealers, find what coarse fishing water is available, and decide which rivers or still waters you want to fish. You can then buy a rod licence and such fishing tickets as may be required. I strongly advise you to join your local angling club or clubs. In this way much water will be thrown open to you with a minimum of trouble.

If you live in a big city or in a highly industrial region there may be very little good coarse fishing water in the immediate area. In this case it is more desirable than ever to join one of the city's clubs, for you will then be able to fish the various waters they control and take advantage of the relatively cheap travelling facilities arranged by the club at weekends.

Armed, then, with a licence to fish, authority to fish, and some tackle and bait you can start your fishing career. Tackle is a

Even during winter freeze-up▲, streams and rivers can continue to provide sport with fish such as these finely-conditioned chub (▼). Legering in the slower water is likely to be the best method.

vitally important matter, but as your choice will to some extent depend on the type of water you intend to fish I will discuss the problem presented by still and running waters before going into the details of choosing tackle.

CHAPTER 2

Types of Water

Fishing water can be divided into two distinct groups, running water and still water. In the first category come rivers and drains, and in the second canals, lakes, reservoirs, ponds and pits. Inside those main divisions many differences demand a different angling approach.

Rivers

There is no limit to the challenges rivers present to the angler. There are long, wide, deep rivers with a moderately fast flow like the Severn and Thames; great but slower rivers like the Trent and Great Ouse; wide fast rivers like the Usk and Wye, primarily salmon and trout rivers but holding a good head of coarse fish in the lower reaches; and there are similar but smaller rivers in the Yorkshire Plain.

There are, too, innumerable smaller rivers and tributaries, some flowing fast and allowing little weed growth, some so sluggish that they are almost choked with aquatic plants.

Each and all of them provide some species of coarse fish with the sort of life they like. Rivers like the Thames and Severn accommodate nearly all species, for the varying character of the long river affords every type of water – still backwaters, swift runs over gravel, and deep pools where the water moves slowly. Smaller rivers have more clearly defined characteristics and will support only a limited number of species.

Drains

Drains in this connection have nothing to do with sewers and are merely surface drainage channels. The Forty Foot in Lincolnshire and the King's Sedgemoor Drain in Somerset are important examples. They are wide, deep, straight cuts through the countryside, designed to take surplus water to the sea.

▲ *A weirpool is one of the most interesting parts of a river to fish, and generally contains better-than-average specimens of all the species to be found in the river.*

▼ *Bream, roach, perch and pike are the principal species to be found in the gently moving waters of Britain's canals.*

Stone-rivetted and turf-banked, they are far more impressive than most canals, though perhaps not so pleasing to the eye.

I have mentioned two outstanding examples, but similar though smaller drains were cut wherever a plain had to be drained. They can be found in large or small sizes in many parts of Lincolnshire, Norfolk, Suffolk, Cheshire, Essex and Somerset.

Since their object is to drain off surplus water there is usually a current. Since they are cut only in almost flat countryside the current is slow. As they pass their surplus water into the sea or a river estuary the outfall is sometimes regulated by a sluice-gate to stop the entry of a rising tide. Some drains, therefore, are almost still for part of the day and have gently flowing water when the gates are opened.

Bream are the predominant fish in drains, with roach a close second. Many hold a good head of pike and in some Fen drains, zander abound.

Canals

There are about 3,000 miles of canal in England and Wales, much of which is administered by British Waterways.

Nearly all of the canals provide fishing, some poor, some good and some of superlative excellence.

Whatever their status, canals are most important fishing waters. The fully maintained canals are not often the best for fishing. Regular weed cutting and persistent barge traffic do not lead to large numbers of big fish.

Canals under some care and maintenance and those recently abandoned provide very good fishing, especially if, in the latter case, a local angling club organises some sensibly-planned weed cutting. Plant growth supports and encourages populations of small creatures which form so large a proportion of the average fish's diet; creatures like water snails, freshwater shrimps, water fleas and the larvae of innumerable species of aquatic flies including bloodworms.

Roach, perch, eels and pike are found in most canals. Rudd

17

are plentiful in many. Bream do well if the canal is a deep one. Well-weeded canals support very good tench and carp, the latter usually the result of stocking.

Towpaths allow the angler easy movement and canals are therefore particularly suited to the wandering methods of angling described in Chapter 4.

Lakes and Ponds

There is no clearly cut distinction between a lake and a pond. An ornamental water an acre in extent in a park may be a lake and the same thing elsewhere may be a pond.

One of the most difficult things in the whole of coarse fishing is finding the fish in large lakes such as Windermere. The newcomer to such a water must trust to luck or local advice.

The small pond offers few problems, for a judicious application of groundbait or loosefeed should draw the fish together.

Between these extremes there is every possible variation of still water – miserable rubbish-filled ponds in which only tench or crucian carp can subsist; well-weeded ponds which allow carp to grow big; and other ponds and lakes which support every still-water species of British fish and sometimes foreign introductions such as zander and catfish.

Reservoirs

Some reservoirs are natural lakes that have been improved and tapped by water undertakings. These usually hold the native coarse fish. Others (and these in the majority) are lakes formed by damming rivers or streams. These are usually stocked with trout, though some reservoirs in and around London are notable exceptions. A few hold both trout and coarse fish.

Pits

Pits are most important coarse fishing waters. They exist in almost every corner of the country and they can provide

Contrasting still-water fisheries. A likely tench swim (▲), reed-fringed but full of snags, and the exposed waters of a big gravel pit (▼), home of large pike. Unfamiliar waters of this size can look featureless, so you should try to get advice from an angler who knows the water about where the best swims are.

Throwing in groundbait at the start of a fishing session. A shoal of bream may require large amounts of groundbait to persuade it to remain in one place, but for other species the best general rule is 'little and often'.

excellent coarse fishing even in the heart of the trout and salmon fishing areas.

They are artificially formed by the removal of some required substance. The common type are clay, sand and gravel pits but many other substances are taken from the ground leaving excavations behind them.

Springs usually fill these holes with water. Angling clubs are alive to the value of pits, most of which are leased and stocked with fish as soon as work on them ceases.

They are usually deep and sometimes very deep. Their area naturally depends on the extent of the workings but most of them fall within the limits of half-an-acre to five acres.

Since they start off empty the species of fish they hold depends entirely upon what their angling sponsors put into them.

CHAPTER 3

Tackle and How to Use It

The essential items of tackle for coarse fishing are rod, reel, line, float, hook and weights. There are many other items, some highly desirable, some luxuries rather than necessities.

There is a very large range of rods and reels, from inexpensive and simply made ones to highly finished articles of high craftsmanship costing a great deal. Later in your angling career you will find one rod and one reel insufficient for your needs, but in your first season I suggest that one of each is enough.

How much you spend on this is a matter for your personal decision, but at this stage I suggest you avoid the really cheap and the really expensive rods and reels. It is sensible to choose only tackle made by well-known manufacturers. Do, if you can, make all your early purchases from a really good tackle shop, one which has a large range of stock and where the proprietor understands about fishing and fishing tackle. If he is a fisherman himself he should also be able to give you advice on the fishing obtainable locally.

For many of you this will be your first fishing season. You do not know yet exactly what sort of angling is going to give the greatest pleasure. As your likes and dislikes harden you are bound to become a specialist of some sort, however wide your tastes.

You may prefer fishing in rivers to still water; you may like big lakes and reservoirs better than ponds and pits. Canals may give you all you require of angling. You may decide that roach fishing is the finest possible sport, or you may enjoy better the entirely different tactics necessary for perch fishing. You may become an enthusiastic match fisherman.

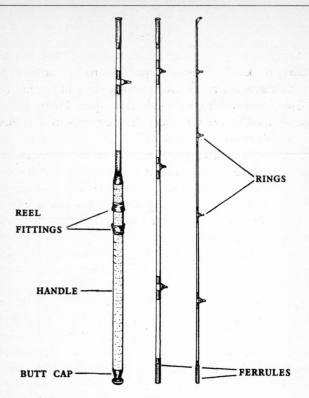

Figure 1   The parts of a coarse fishing rod

There will be some compromises which need to be made when you are looking at choices and you are unlikely to come to quite such clear-cut conclusions, but the point is that you will develop some preferences.

Different species of fish, waters and methods of fishing demand different tackle; and until you have found out what you like doing best it would be unwise to spend a great deal of money on rods and reels. Once you do know, you can spend money wisely on buying better quality tackle that exactly suits your needs.

Rods

Nowadays most rods are made from carbon fibre and this is certainly the kind to choose for your first rod. It combines lightness with strength to an extent which none of the more old-fashioned rod-making materials can equal. However, always remember, DO NOT fish under electricity pylons or in thunder storms with carbon rods or poles.

It will help you decide what sort of rod you should buy if you think about the sort of job which a rod has to do. You use it to cast – to project your tackle out into the water. When a fish bites you use it to strike: you raise the tip of the rod to tighten the line and set the hook. Then the rod helps you to play the fish: it is strong enough to enable you to keep pressure on the fish and at the same time, by bending, it absorbs the force of sudden plunges by the fish which might otherwise break the line.

Specialised rods tend to perform one function extra well at the expense of others. Thus the prime function of a match rod is to enable you to strike extremely quickly when float fishing for shy-biting fish, whereas the prime function of a carp rod is to control a large, powerful fish in its struggles to escape. For your first season, what you should buy is a *general purpose* rod, one which will carry out the three functions described above for the range of fishing methods you are likely to use and the range of species and sizes of fish you are likely to catch. A 12ft rod is a useful all-round length. It may seem at first that a shorter rod would be easier to manage, but the longer rod has advantages, especially for float fishing. The owner of your local tackle shop will be able to advise you.

Although modern carbon fibre rods require less special care than rods made from other materials, nevertheless you must look after your rod if you want it to last. Make sure that both it and its storage bag are dry before you put it away, and then either hang it up by the loop at the end of the bag or lay it flat on a shelf: never leave a rod leaning against a wall. Ideally, and when you can afford it, your rods will be kept in a special holdall available from tackle shops.

Reels

Nowadays the fixed-spool reel is almost universally used for coarse fishing, and has effectively superseded the traditional centre-pin reel. However it is a fairly complex mechanism, and it is important that you learn how to use it properly.

Fixed-spool Reels

You can buy a good fixed-spool reel for around £30. Choose one for which you can get spare spools; as you gain experience you may want to take more than one strength of line with you when you go fishing.

Figure 2 shows a simple form of fixed-spool reel. The hollow spool holds the line. At the rear of most reels you will find the drag knob. This puts the spool under tension and can be

A modern fixed-spool reel. Note the drag knob at the rear, used to adjust spool tension.

adjusted to the strength of line being used. Curved over the spool is the wire-like pick-up arm. When you turn the handle the arm (known as the bale arm) rotates around the spool, gathering in the line and distributing it evenly onto the spool.

Modern reels have varying rates of retrieval, and some designed for winding in your end tackle quickly during matches can be as fast at 6:1.

It is, of course, an excellent idea to watch someone using a fixed-spool reel and, if possible, to try a cast or two with it before you buy one.

Having bought a reel try the following experiments.

1. Put the line on the reel (see '**Lines**' below).

2. Go out-of-doors, put the reel on the rod and thread the line through the rings.

3. Tie an object weighing about 6 oz to the line and lay it on the ground. *Do not attempt to cast this or to raise it clear of the ground with the rod.*

Stand about 12 yards back, with the rod raised at an angle of 45 degrees to 50 degrees. Hold the handle of the rod in your right hand with the reel support between the second and third fingers. Set the tension screw at its lightest. With the bale arm in the engaged position, reel in. You will find that you cannot draw the object along the ground because the drag is slipping and giving line. Do not persist in this experiment, for each turn of the handle puts a twist in the line in these conditions.

4. Try the same thing with different settings of the tension until the drag no longer slips. You can then draw the weight along the ground.

5. With the tension again set as lightly as possible, lower the rod to a horizontal position. Drop your first finger to the moving part of the reel and hold it. Now raise the rod slowly to about 50 degrees. Line cannot escape and the weight comes along the ground.

Figure 2   Casting with a fixed-spool reel. Note that the reel is mounted near the top of the rod handle. (a) Starting position, with the rod held across the body and the pick-up arm of the reel in the open position. The detailed drawing shows how the right hand should grip the rod handle, with the forefinger retaining the line. (b) The cast in progress: the rod now points ahead of the angler and the line has been released and is flying out. In swinging the rod from (a) to (b) the forearm moves forward and away from the body, but the main impetus is imparted by the wrist. The detailed drawing shows the position of the forefinger immediately after releasing the line, which is beginning to peel off the spool.

(c) and (d) show alternative starting positions, which can be useful if there are bushes or other obstructions on the bank.

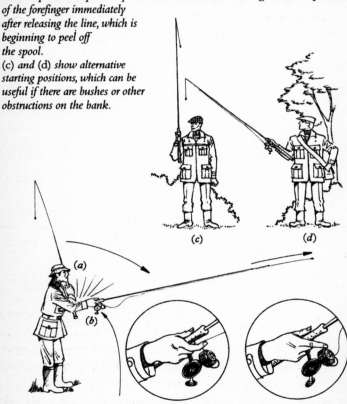

Take your finger off the reel and with the left hand reel in as you lower the rod again to the horizontal, thus recovering the line gained by raising the rod. Repeat this process until the weight is a yard or two away. This process is known as pumping.

When you hook a fish that exerts no more pressure than the setting of the tension it can be played on the reel as in 4 above. When you hook anything stronger, you must use the pumping method as in 5 above.

Even with sufficient tension, finger control on the reel is advisable, and it should always be used when a fish is being brought over the net.

Practise. Take your rod and tackle to an open piece of ground.

Tie a ¼ oz (4 dram) non-toxic weight to the end of the line. A weight which will not readily get caught up in the grass is best, such as an Arlesey bomb, or drilled bullet.

Reel up until the weight dangles about 2 ft from the tip of the rod.

Hold the rod with the right hand, with the reel standard between second and third fingers.

Trap the line by letting it lie across the tip of the first finger between reel and rod. Raise the bale arm.

Hold the rod across your body to the left at an angle of about 45 degrees to the ground. Bring it forward and a little upwards with a smooth motion. Just before the rod points straight in front of you release the line from your finger. Halt the rod as it points to your front.

If all has gone well, the line should be flying off the spool and the weight descending some distance away in front of you.

Turn the handle (which will automatically engage the bale arm) and reel in.

Having made a couple of haphazard casts like this, continue to practise.

Try to gauge exactly the strength of your casting. With a

27

fixed-spool reel it is easier to cast a long (but uncontrolled) distance than it is to drop your bait exactly, say, 12 yards away.

Distance is controlled partially by the strength of the cast, but is materially aided by the first finger. If you see that your bait is going too far, drop the finger until the line rubs against it. Friction slows the line down. In an emergency (e.g., if you see your hook is going to land in a bush on the opposite bank) clamp a finger to the rim of the reel.

If the field or patch of ground you have chosen is extensive try some long overhead casts. Finger control and general manipulation are the same but the rod tip is brought in an arc from a position behind the back to an angle of some 50 degrees in front.

I have used the expression 'strength of a cast'. No physical strength need be exerted. The wrist puts the rod through its motion and the rod does the work.

Having attained some mastery of distance, concentrate on direction. Put out targets (e.g., small squares of paper held down with stones) at varying distances in different directions and try to land your weight on them.

Fishing with a Fixed-spool Reel. When you arrive at the waterside, set up your rod, reel and line and attach whatever end tackle you intend to use (see Chapter 4).

Bait up and cast. When you get a bite and the time comes to strike, put your first finger on the drum to hold the line and strike.

Raise the finger the instant you feel the hook is driven home. Keep the rod at about 60 degrees.

In a few seconds you will know roughly the size of fish you are connected with.

If it is a small one it can be reeled towards the bank, lifted and swung in. If it is a fish that is likely to need the landing net, play it more carefully, having the first finger always ready to assist the reel by braking it. If the fish is something exceptional, play it entirely by braking with the finger and pumping, letting the fish go when it wants to run but exerting as much pressure as you think is safe. If it seems likely that the fish will gain a weed bed or other snag, give no line, and lower the rod to about 45 degrees so that the strain is evenly distributed along its length and not left to the top joint.

When the fish is exhausted, pump it towards the bank. With a finger on the drum, draw the fish over the landing net.

General Hints. Never try to *reel* in a fish that is swimming away from you. Slow it and eventually stop it by the finger-on-the-drum technique.

Never reel slack line on to a fixed-spool reel or it will go where it shouldn't! After a cast, take up slack by raising the rod before you reel in. If you have too much slack out to do this, rest the butt of the rod against your body, put your right hand six inches or more above the reel and let the line run between two fingers as you reel in with the left hand. This keeps the line taut and prevents loose coils twisting around handles, the reel itself, etc.

Do not use too heavy a line (see '**Lines**', below) or it will tend to come off the reel in coils.

Always look down at the reel when you have completed a cast, laid the rod on its rest, or touched it in any way. *Make this an automatic habit with every type of reel.* Its object is to see that the line runs freely from reel to first ring and has not caught round reel or rod.

Advantages of Fixed-spool Reels. The greatest advantage the beginner gains from using a fixed-spool reel is the ability to cast light tackle, including the lightest of float tackle, as far as he is likely to want without difficulty. Correct control of the reel when a fish has been hooked calls for practice and experience.

Centre-pin Reels
The centre-pin is by far the older type of reel, and some anglers still prefer it for long-trotting. Most recently, some anglers have

A centre-pin reel.

found it a very useful tool for close-in fishing on the many pools which hold small carp.

Centre-pins are precision instruments which can cost a great deal of money, with top of the range models reaching £250. They will not generally be used by the beginner and are best left until later in your angling career.

Lines

By far the most popular line is nylon monofilament. You will see in advertisements and hear anglers talking about monofilament, monofil, mono, and nylon; and all mean the same thing. Nylon is the word commonly used and I mention this because it should not be confused with *braided* nylon, a very different type of line.

Nylon Monofilament

Produced in different colours, and a variety of strengths (known as breaking strains), there are many British and continental brands on the market.

It is made in breaking strains from about 12 oz (for the finest coarse fishing) to 100 lb (for heavy sea fishing).

Most makes are sold on spools holding 100, 50 or 25 metres but spools of bulk line can also be bought.

It is slightly elastic, the amount of elasticity varying in different makes.

Knots. It is inclined to slip when tied by simple knots and
several tested knots are recommended for it. To avoid complication I have illustrated only two. *Figure 3(a)* shows how to tie a
loop. The half-blood knot [*Figure 3(b)*] can be used for almost
every other purpose such as tying a line or cast to a loop or the
eye of a hook; tying the line to the drum of the reel before
winding on the line; and tying the line or cast to a leger or
paternoster weight. Several manufacturers issue free cards or
booklets giving knots for and notes about nylon monofilament.

What to Buy. I suggest that you gradually test different
brands of nylon monofilament until you find the one you like
working with best. Avoid those which seem comparatively stiff
and wiry. A good start can be made with 100 yards of 3 lb breaking strain nylon. This will give good all-round service but is too
heavy for delicate fishing. However, you can get any degree of

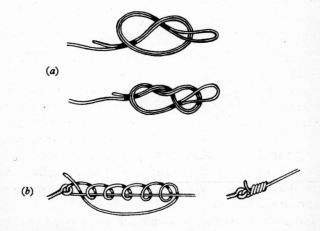

(a)

(b)

*Figure 3   (a) Loop knot suitable for nylon monofilament, and (b) the
half-blood knot. All knots should first be moistened (if you do this in your
mouth be careful of hooks) and then drawn gently tight.*

Figure 4   A correctly filled spool (left), *an under-filled spool* (centre) *and an over-filled spool* (right). *If you have too little line on your reel it will not peel freely off the spool and will restrict the distance of your casts. With too much, loops of line tend to slip off behind the spool and cause tangles.*

fineness you want by using hook-lengths (see below) of lesser breaking strain.

In order to get the best casting service from a fixed-spool reel it must be filled almost to the top rim of the spool. *Almost,* but not quite. Keep the line a match thickness below the rim, or coils of line are likely to slip off and be a nuisance.

Centre-pin reels also need to be fairly well filled with line to get the best out of them. The more line you have on the reel the greater is the circumference of the drum and, consequently the rate of line recovery. If you do not have enough new line to fill up the reel adequately, you can make up the difference with 'backing' – old, unreliable line or very fine string. Although it is rather tedious, there is only one way to gauge exactly how much backing you need, which is as follows. First wind your new line onto the reel, and then put on enough backing to fill the reel up to the correct point. Then reverse the line and back-ing; you can do this by laying them out on a stretch of open ground and winding them back onto the reel, starting with the backing.

Winding Line on the Reel. Nearly all brands of nylon monofilament are sold on spools. Transfer of line from spool to reel can cause endless trouble if it is not done correctly.

Put a pencil or any other suitable axle through the hole in the spool and fix its ends firmly so that the spool revolves freely.

Two large books closed on to the ends make effective holders for the axle.

Fix the reel on the handle of your rod. Disconnect the end of the line from the spool and tie it to the drum of the reel, using the half-blood knot.

Now wind the line on to the reel, distributing it evenly. In the case of a fixed-spool reel keep the right hand round the rod well above the reel and let the line run through the fingers exerting enough pressure to keep it reasonably taut. *The spool from which you are taking line must revolve.* If you wind on coils as they come off the side of an inert spool you will put enough kinks in the line to make fishing impossible.

Besides the method just described, there are several gadgets on the market which hold the spool of line and clip to the butt of the rod. They are intended to make loading your reel easier, but only buy these if you can afford them. Money spent on these could be better saved for more important gear like hooks, floats etc.

Precaution. Snip two or three feet off the end of the line after a day's fishing. It may have weakened. Every week or so test the last few yards of the line. Nylon can deteriorate quite suddenly along its entire length, and when this happens it must be replaced. It is asking for disaster to fish with a suspect line.

Figure 5   Disposing of unwanted nylon.

Special Note. There will be many occasions at the waterside when you find you have useless lengths of nylon monofilament. You may have had a breakage or cut off a yard or two of kinked line. *Never throw away waste nylon.* Wind it round two fingers and cut it into 2 in lengths. Birds easily get entangled in it and then starve to death. Small birds like wrens and tits can get into trouble with as little as 6 or 8 in lengths – so dispose of it all safely in the bin at home.

Braided Lines

These are lines of braided natural materials such as silk or cotton (now virtually obsolete) or manufactured products such as nylon and terylene.

I have already suggested that you use a nylon monofilament line for all purposes during your first fishing season. A few anglers use braided terylene for lure fishing because it is very supple but this is something you can make up your mind about later in your angling career. Braided lines are considerably more expensive than monofilament.

Hooks

Figure 6 is a rough scale of hook sizes for coarse fishing, rough because there is no agreed standard and hooks of the same number may vary slightly with pattern and source of origin.

The sizes of hooks to use for different purposes are recommended in the chapters on bait and fishes.

Loose hooks can be bought with or without eyes – the latter sort being called spade-end hooks. To begin with, buy eyed hooks since these are easier to tie on. Always get them with straight eyes – not turned up or turned down.

Buy a good brand of hooks. The small savings you can make by buying cheap hooks simply are not worth it, since an inferior hook will probably break or straighten as soon as you hook a good fish.

Hooks-to-nylon are eyeless hooks professionally tied to short (8 in to 20 in) lengths of nylon monofilament. They are

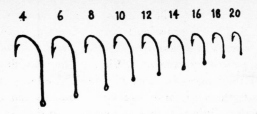

Figure 6   Hook sizes: the pattern illustrated is Crystal bend, the most popular all-round pattern for coarse fishing.

convenient to use in the smaller sizes, but are appreciably more expensive than eyed hooks so that you will probably decide that it is worth buying the eyed kind and tying them on yourself.

Hook-length. This is the short length of nylon to which a hook-to-nylon is fastened. If you do buy hooks-to-nylon, note the breaking strain of the nylon printed on the packet and ensure that it is lower than the breaking strain of your reel-line. Then if you lose a hook in an underwater snag you will lose only the hook and not several feet of your reel-line and perhaps your float as well.

For the same reason it is a good idea to tie your eyed hooks to lower breaking strain hook-lengths if there are snags where

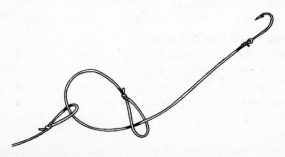

Figure 7   Attaching a hook-length to the reel-line.

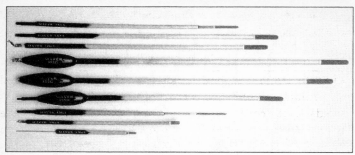

A selection of straight and bodied wagglers for rivers and still waters.

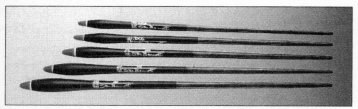

Various lengths of balsa stick float used for trotting in running water.

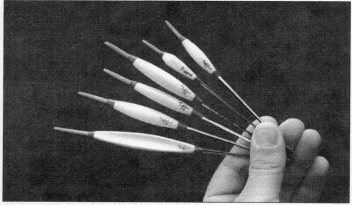

'Topper' floats, named after well-known angler Mervyn 'Topper' Haskins. These are used for trotting turbulent swims at long range.

you are fishing. You can also fish finer for wary fish without having to carry several different strengths of reel-line. Buy nylon for hook-lengths in 100 m spools, each of which should last a long time.

Tie a loop at the end of your line and another at the end of the hook-length. Then join them together as shown in *Figure 9*.

Floats

On your first visit to a tackle shop you will probably be amazed at the hundreds of different floats on the market. Most anglers build up a fair collection over the years, but for a beginner, there is only the need for a handful to start with. I would suggest a couple of peacock wagglers, an insert and bodied waggler and a couple of stick floats. A sliding float is also a good idea if you plan to fish water deeper than the length of your rod. It also pays to have rubber float adaptors so you can change your float without dismantling your rig.

I have mentioned these in Chapter 4, but I suggest that float-less legering or paternostering are often better in such circumstances. If you do decide to use a sliding float, find the depth at which you want to fish and tie a piece of nylon around the line at that point to act as a stop-knot. Snip off the ends to about ⅙ in. This will stop the float running higher up the line, but the nylon stop will go through the rod rings.

When you are ready to cast, the slider float will rest on the first of your split shot. When the bait reaches the water the weights take it down and the line runs through the rings of the float, which remains on the surface. When the top ring of the float comes into contact with the nylon stop the line is halted and the bait is suspended at the required depth.

Weights

Split shot. The most useful weights for coarse fishing with floats are split shot. These are small non-toxic metal spheres with an open slit in them. The line is put in the slit and the shot squeezed until it closes. This can be (and all too often is) done with the teeth, but a pair of pliers is better.

Split shot are usually sold in tins or boxes containing an assortment of sizes. The largest are known as swan shot, the smallest as dust shot. If you can, buy soft shot (recognisable by their grey colour as opposed to the near-black of hard shot); these are less likely to damage the line when you squeeze them on. *Figure 9(a)* shows three swan shots threaded on to a loop of nylon. The strength of the current will determine how many shots you will need.

Leger weights. There are many shapes and sizes. Three of the most useful kinds are illustrated in *Figure 9*, and their use is further described under '**Leger Fishing**' in Chapter 4.

The size of weight you need will depend on the strength of the current and the distance you have to cast. Use the *lightest* that will answer the purpose.

Landing Nets

I did not include a landing net amongst the essential requirements for coarse fishing, but without one you can suffer disappointment and frustration as well as possibly injuring the fish. When you have hooked and played your fish you have to land it. Where there is shallow water which you can reach it is often possible to beach a fish and pick it up by its tail or gills, but in the majority of places there will be steep banks or borders of reeds.

Fish of a few ounces can be swung in without bother, but an attempt to lift heavier fish will probably result in a broken line. It may also strain the rod.

Fishing tackle dealers can show you several designs. Avoid short-handled ones. Light telescopic handles are best and can be bought fairly cheaply. The net should be 15 inches or more in diameter for general coarse fishing. If going after large pike, carp, barbel or catfish you'll need a proper specimen net, but these can be expensive.

When fishing, have the landing net within reach. When you have hooked and played a sizeable fish slip the net into the water and draw the fish over it. Raise the net and bring it in. If the fish is a very heavy one let the ground take some of its weight as you bring in the net.

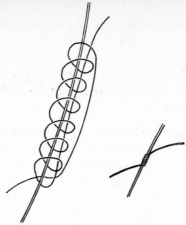

Figure 8   *Stop knot for use with a sliding float: tied thus it will slide easily through the rod rings but not through the small eye on the float.*

(a)   *(b)*   *(c)*   *(d)*

Figure 9   *Weights:* (a) *Swan shot link: this most versatile of leger weights consists of swan shots pinched onto a loop of nylon, the number of shots being varied to suit the strength of the current.* (b) *The Arlesey bomb: its streamlined shape is ideal for distance casting.* (c) *The coffin weight's flattened shape is useful for fishing over soft mud in which other weights tend to become buried. However, since the line passes right through the weight it may offer more resistance to a taking fish than either* (a) *or* (d)*.* (d) *The swimfeeder consists of a short plastic tube with a non-toxic strip attached, and is often used instead of an ordinary weight for legering in rivers. The tube is filled with a mixture of hookbait and groundbait, which trickles out onto the bed of the river, attracting the fish. A swimfeeder is cumbersome to cast and should not be used in shallow swims, where the splash will frighten the fish. Note the piece of valve rubber threaded on immediately below the swimfeeder to act as a buffer. It is still permissible to use lead weights of under 0.06 grams and over 28.35 grams (1 oz).*

Miscellaneous Items

Disgorgers

These are plastic tubes around six inches long, for removing hooks too far down to reach with the fingers. Every angler should have at least two of these in their box in case the fish swallows the bait. It is vital to carry out unhooking of this nature as quickly as possible and with the minimum amount of stress to the fish.

Keep Nets

You will find a keep net essential if you ever go in for match fishing. They are used to keep the catch alive until the weigh-in at the end of the match. Some anglers like to use them in pleasure fishing so they can survey their catch at the end of the day before returning fish to the water.

Figure 10   Landing net with extending handle

Figure 11   Keep net for retaining fish until the end of the day.

Using the landing net: the net should be sunk into the water and the fish drawn over it. Never jab at the fish with the net, as you will probably either knock it off the hook or else provoke a last-minute struggle for freedom.

A keep net consists of a long sleeve of netting kept open by a series of rings. The top end is pegged firmly to the bank and the body of the net lies in the water.

Line Floatants

In ordinary float fishing and even more so in long-trotting the line *must* float. Line floatant is sold in tins. Brands containing silicones are excellent. Smear a fold of cloth with floatant, hold it between thumb and finger and draw the line slowly through the fold.

Rod Rests

There are many styles of rod rests, but all you will need to start with are two or three threaded banksticks with removable rubber or plastic heads.

Swivels

Swivels are used extensively in spinning and pike fishing, and are designed to prevent twist accumulating in the line. A swivel consists of a small metal sleeve with an eye at each end, each eye being free to rotate independently of the other.

Oddments

Some other handy items are: a fishing bag if you plan to take a roving approach or a seat box to sit on and carry your smaller items. A comfortable angler will always be able to concentrate better.

A towel to wipe your hands, and scissors for cutting line and trimming knots are also useful.

Fishing Methods

I shall discuss in this chapter the well-proven and successful methods of bait fishing, but for the benefit of complete beginners I will first describe a routine, applicable to nearly all methods of fishing, which may be helpful as a guide. It can be (and should be) modified to suit your own temperament and any special local conditions.

When you arrive at the fishing place do not go straight to the water's edge. Put down your burdens some distance back and then make a close study of the water (treading softly, moving slowly and making every possible use of cover) and decide where you are going to fish.

Establish a base a few yards from the bank on which to unpack your kit.

Tackling Up

Take the rod from its bag and put the bag in a safe place. It does not matter where, but develop a habit of always putting it in the *same* place.

Put the rod together. With a 3-piece rod fit the top and middle joint first, adding the butt section last.

See that the rod rings are exactly in line.

If there is no ring on the butt section see that the reel fitting is in line with the rings on the other sections.

Fix the reel on the handle by means of the metal reel- or winch-fittings. With a fixed-spool reel the spool of line should be forward – i.e., nearest the rod rings. With a centre-pin reel the handles should be on the right.

Pull off about 1½ rod-lengths of line from the reel. The line from a centre-pin reel should run to the rod rings from the *bottom* of the reel. Thread the line through the rings. Check to see that you have not missed a ring. The fault is easily corrected at this stage but if you discover it later it means dismantling float, hook, leads, etc., to put it right.

Thread your float (or float adaptor) onto your line and as a rule set it using split shot at about four feet from the hook. Now add the hook-length or tie the hook if it is an eyed pattern.

Important Note

While tackling up the safest place for your rod is in the rod rests which hopefully you have bought. If you have no rests, lean the rod over your bag or box.

Untackling

When you have finished fishing for the day, remove the hook-length by cutting the line just above the knot, and take it home with you.

Take off the float and shot.

Reel in the line and take the reel off the rod.

Disconnect the top joint of the rod from the middle one, and then the middle from the butt.

Wipe the rod sections with a piece of dry cloth and put the rod back in its bag.

Note

The methods of fishing which follow describe only the way to arrange tackle and its general use. Such details as the depth at which to fish, the baits to use or when to strike will be found in Chapter 7, where fishing for different species of fish is discussed.

Float Fishing

Float fishing is a wide subject, for by ringing the changes on floats, shotting and depth in still and running water an immense number of different combinations is possible.

I deal here with float fishing in still and running water, long trotting, laying on, and 'wander' fishing.

In all forms of float fishing it is essential to know the exact depth of the water at the actual fishing point. This can be found

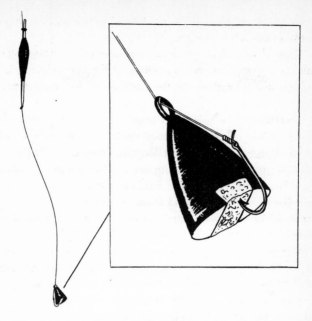

Figure 12 A plummet is used for finding the depth of the water.
Detail: *the hook is stuck into a cork strip running along the bottom of the plummet.*

by using the plummet (*Figure 12*) or, in still water, by putting just enough weight on the hook to sink the float. A small pierced bullet will usually be sufficient for this and will cause less disturbance than a heavy plummet. If the float lies flat on the surface bring it down the line. If it sinks, bring it up the line. The second cast should be roughly correct and a third will make it exact. Once you know the depth, adjust the float so that the bait fishes where you want it.

In Still Water

No water is really still because winds and convection always cause some movement, but it is a useful expression which embraces lakes, reservoirs, ponds, pits and most canals.

Simple float fishing in any of these waters follows the same general principles.

Select your fishing point, taking advantage of cover. Try to get down behind reeds and rushes, alongside or in front of a bush, or in the shadow of a tree. If there is no cover keep well back from the bank.

When you have assembled your tackle at the rear base, bring forward to the fishing point everything you are likely to need – rod, small spares such as hook-lengths, floats, casts, shot, etc., rod rests, baits, ground-bait, landing net, and whatever you intend to sit on. Spare rods, reels, tackle, food etc. can be left in the rear, but since your object is to avoid frequent movement, make certain you have all you want for an hour or two in your forward position.

Find the depth, adjust your float, bait the hook and cast in. Just as the float and tackle are about to hit the water, brake the line with your finger as it comes off the reel. This will prevent the float and shot entering the water in a bunch and thereby making a splash which could frighten the fish.

Deep Water. The foregoing is a straightforward method in many ponds, lakes and canals when you will be fishing in a depth not greater than the length of the rod. If you fish deep in pits, reservoirs or lakes you will have to use a sliding float, but legering (see below) is usually a better method in such circumstances.

Clear Shallows. In clear shallow water (common conditions on canals) it is advisable to sit well to the left or right of the chosen fishing spot and cast to it, thus increasing the distance between you and the fish. In such conditions the fish can see you and your movements right across the width of the normal canal. The finest of tackle is necessary with the smallest possible float.

Sinking the Bait. You will often find that small fry occupy the near-surface waters and seize your bait before it has time to sink to the better fish that you hope are waiting below. When this happens, add more weight near the hook length in order to sink the bait quickly. When there are no small fish about, try putting a shot just below the float (sufficient to cock it), fishing without other weight. The baited hook sinks slowly and naturally and may often be taken on its way down.

Defeating Wind. A strong wind can be a nuisance in most forms of fishing and is particularly so in still water. Instead of the placid conditions where your float stays where you put it you find that the wind affects float and line and forces them into the bank or further out into the water where the depth may be wrong and your groundbait does not influence the fish.

In these circumstances put enough shot on your line to sink the float until only the least visible tip remains above the surface. This offers little resistance to the wind.

Better still, you can use an antenna float, which is specially designed to offer little resistance to the wind – since the bulky part of the body is submerged and acts as a stabiliser – and yet remains readily visible to the angler.

In Running Water

In still water the angler casts, his float remains where it falls and he can (and in carp and tench fishing often does) remain without further action for an hour or more. In running water the float is never still. As soon as it reaches the water it and the sinking hook and bait are borne downstream by the current. This demands an entirely different fishing technique.

Fishing the Swim. This is the most popular method of river float fishing. The swim is the water you can cover with your tackle from your fixed position. To fish the swim you cast upstream and allow the float to travel past your front and downstream to the limit of the length of line you have chosen to use.

Do not be too ambitious to begin with. Keep to a length of line you can manage with ease until you have thoroughly mastered the technique.

47

The following is the usual sequence of action.

1.   Select a swim. When you get to know a river you will learn where the best swims are. On new water try to find a clear run between beds of weed, or a swim on the deeper side of a ledge where the bankside shallows suddenly deepen.

2.   Find the exact depth of the swim.

3.   Settle down comfortably with all you need around you.

4.   Throw a ball of groundbait upstream — *in exact line with your swim* — to a point where you think it will reach the bottom near the upstream end of your swim. In deeper water mix your groundbait more firmly so it will break up later rather than sooner.

5.   Adjust your float to the required depth. The usual aim is to allow the bait to travel along just off the bottom — or 'tripping along the bottom' as it is often described. Shotting plays an important part in this. In a slight current the arrangement shown in *Figure 13(b)* or *(e)* can be tried. In a stronger stream heavier weighting is required [*Figure 13(c)*] in order to sink the bait quickly to the bottom and to keep it there.

The distance between float and hook should be a little greater than the actual depth, for the current bears the line downstream at a slant, while the unweighted hook length tends to swing up.

6.   Decide what length of line you are going to use and cast upstream so that float and tackle fall gently at the top of the selected swim. Turn the reel handle to engage the bale arm.

As the float comes towards you, keep the line reasonably taut by raising the rod. When the float has passed you, give up line (at a rate dictated by the current) by lowering the rod.

7.   When lowering the rod, do so in such a way as to check the float *very slightly* so that the bait travels ahead of it. It is better to use too light than too heavy a touch. In the latter case the bait

▲ *The roach.* ▼ *The bream.*

▲ *The chub.* ▼ *The perch.*

▲ *The tench.*

▼ *This lovely olive-flanked tench was the result of an early summer's morning session.*

▲ *The dace.*   ▼ *A fine brace of crucian carp taken on float tackle.*

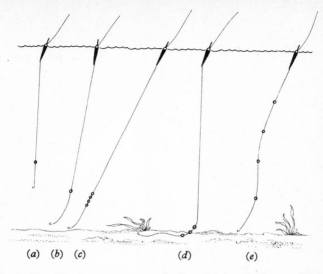

Figure 13   Shotting arrangements for float fishing. The function of the different arrangements are explained in the text. Try to avoid using a larger float than necessary and use enough shot: no more of the float should show above water than is necessary for you to see it properly.

will rise from the bottom and the float may veer out of the swim towards the bank.

8.   When the float reaches the end of its allotted swim allow it to remain there for 10 or 15 seconds. The force of the current raises the bait in an arc from the bottom to, perhaps, mid-water, and it is often taken by a fish as it rises.

9.   Let the current swing the halted float out of the current, retrieve enough line to enable you to raise line, float and hook from the water by raising the rod, and cast the whole lot upstream again for the next run. With a little practice these motions become automatic.

Let me repeat: do not be too ambitious to start with. Be content to use a short length of line that can be controlled by the rod alone. When you have mastered this technique you can begin to increase the distance your float travels in the following way. After casting in, leave the bale arm in the open position and rest your finger on the spool to prevent line coming off. (If at this stage you have a bite, you must strike while keeping your finger clamped to the spool and then immediately engage the bale.) After the float has passed you, you allow it to continue to travel downstream by lifting your finger from the spool and letting the float draw line off the reel. After a few yards – the exact distance depends on the strength of the current and on how far out from the bank your swim is – the pressure of the current on the line will begin to drag the float off course towards your bank. When this happens, engage the pick-up, allow the float to swing round out of the swim, reel in and cast again.

Under special circumstances it is possible to trot the tackle a long way downstream, a technique known as long-trotting using a stick float.

Long-trotting

Long-trotting is a special form of float fishing which often proves more successful than any other. Unfortunately the types of water in which it can be practised are limited.

The essential requirement is a river with a fairly fast-moving current – anything, say, from 2 miles an hour upwards.

In favourable circumstances long-trotting can be done from the bank and it is a killing method. I shall refer to it later in this section.

Long-trotting is only an extension of 'fishing the swim'. There you 'trotted' a bait along the bottom by constant casting. In long-trotting you let the current do the work for you. The advantages lie in the word 'long'. Unless you do something silly – like drumming with your heels on the bank – you send your bait down to completely unsuspicious fish that cannot possibly see you, thus overcoming the greatest hazard that besets every sort of angling.

Presume that the main current of a river holds, among other fish, chub, dace, and roach – three species to which long-trotting

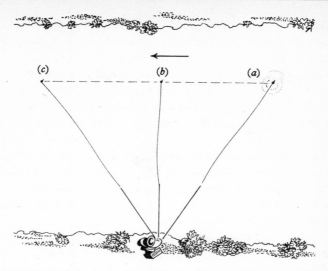

Figure 14   Fishing the swim with float tackle. Cast to a and keep the rod pointing at the float as it travels down the swim, raising the rod as the float approaches b. Always keep the line as taut as possible without actually dragging the float off course.

is especially suited, though fish of several other species may be caught. This is the sequence to follow.

1.   Throw a cricket-ball sized lump of rather loosely moulded groundbait about 10 yards downstream. The groundbait breaks up and is washed down the river. Small particles may go a long way. In favourable fishing conditions the result is that fish gradually move upstream to the source of the food. See also Chapter 6 about additions to groundbait.

2.   Find the depth.

3.   Adjust the float so that the hook is a little further from the float than the depth of the water. It is difficult to lay down exact measures because everything depends on speed of current and depth of river. The bait must be close to the bottom in its passage downstream and a little experience will tell you when it is touching the bottom from time to time – the ideal to aim at.

55

A strong current will need a good deal of weight which in turn will need a buoyant float to sustain it. The shotting shown in *Figure 13(c)* is the general idea, though the number need not be limited to four. I prefer a small non-toxic weight in strong currents, for this not only takes the place of shot but minimises the twist likely to be put in the line when it is reeled back. Whatever the weight it should be between 12 in and 18 in from the hook.

The float must be buoyant enough to take the weight and big enough to be easily seen at a distance. On the other hand it must not be bulky or too much disturbance will be created on its recovery. An 8 or 9 in balsa stick will do. You must be able to see the float at least 50 yards away and for this purpose I paint the tops of mine a light orange colour. Different eyes see colours differently. It is worth while finding out what colour your eyes see best at 50 yards and painting the tops of all your floats that colour.

4.   Bait the hook and *lower* (do not cast) the end tackle into the water. The current takes it away and you let it run downstream, retarding the float a little (as described in 'fishing the swim') in order to let the baited hook fish ahead of the float.

The ideal reel for long-trotting is a very free running centre-pin or a close face reel. The current will take off line at exactly the right speed. If the reel does not run freely enough or if the line tends to stick on the coils give it encouragement every few seconds by easing the reel rim forward with the finger. The whole principle in this method of fishing lies in the bait moving at exactly the same speed as the current with the float very slightly retarded. There is no allowance for constant halts or yards of loose line.

However your fixed-spool reel will also do the job perfectly well, and the way to use it is as follows. Raise the bale arm and leave it in the free position. The line runs freely off the spool as the current takes the float down. Let it run over the top joint of the first finger. The key skill is to let the line run off at exactly the right speed, without allowing any slack line to build up on the water. When the float indicates a bite, clamp the line to the rod with the first finger and strike. Let go immediately, drop the pick-up, and play the fish in the normal way.

5.   Let the float go down at least 40 yards, and as much more as the nature of the river and your eyesight allow. Halt the line when the float has reached the end of the run. This firstly raises the bait off the river bed; you should be especially alert for a bite at this moment.

6.   It then swings the float out of the swim into slacker water to left or right. This movement is aided by swinging the rod over in the desired direction. Reel in slowly until you can raise the tackle off the water with the rod. This recovery of line through the side waters does not disturb the swim.

7.   Examine the hook, rebait if necessary, and start again.

Long-trotting from the Bank. The same principle is followed throughout, but you must choose your position with care. You need a fairly swift current close inshore. It does not matter if the current swings out further down, but it should be under your rod tip to start with. Rocks, promontories, jetties and anything that juts into the current are good positions for long-trotting.

In favourable circumstances the method can be used to reach shoals of fish that are lying under overhanging shrubs. Choose the first clear patch of bank upstream and trot your hook down to the fish. If they are in relatively slack water (often the case with chub) let your float travel down with the current until it has run the correct distance. Then hold the line. The current should wash the float into the slack water where the fish are lying.

Laying-on

This is a static method of float fishing. Shot are put on the line about 18 in from the hook in such a way that they just rest on the bottom [*Figure 13(d)*]. It is particularly useful in rivers with a sluggish current and in still water when there is a strong wind.

Roving Fishing

This simply means that you wander around, fishing every likely-looking spot.

Ordinary float tackle is used, adjusted to the average depth you will be fishing.

It is an interesting way of fishing waters where movement is easy – canals with towpaths, lakes with open banks, etc., for you travel light, carrying only a bag with spare items of small tackle and your bait. No groundbait is used.

It is a good method for perch at all times and seasons, for chub in summer, and for nearly all species of fish in river flood conditions. In this last case the bait should be dropped into backwaters, eddies and any area protected from the main flood current.

Leger Fishing

Leger fishing is normally done without a float.

The ideal rod for legering is called a quiver-tip, and has one, two or sometimes three different tips to show delicate pulls from the fish. If you cannot afford a quiver-tip, try a bobbin (lump of bread paste or washing-up liquid bottle top) on the line, between the reel and the first ring on the rod. This will show a run by rising, or a drop-back bite by falling.

Thread the line through a bored weight sufficiently heavy to hold the bottom. After the hook is tied on, pinch a split shot on to the line on the hook side of the leger weight about 2 ft from the hook (*Figure 15*). This stops the leger weight from sliding down too near the hook.

A fish that takes the bait can draw line through the leger weight without feeling any resistance. On this account it can be a deadly method of fishing in almost any circumstances, but it is particularly useful for fishing on the bottom in a current and for fishing deep water and distant water.

Figure 15   Legering rig, using a coffin weight. A shot pinched onto the line prevents the weight from sliding down too close to the hook.

As there is no float, any depth of water can be fished. The relatively heavy lead makes long casting possible.

There are many sorts of leger weights, of which the most useful are illustrated in *Figure 9*. Any sort of weight with a metal ring into can be used for legering, the line being threaded through the ring instead of through the weight itself.

When the tackle has been satisfactorily arranged, bait the hook and cast out to the desired spot. Allow the weight to settle and then reel in until the line is nearly taut.

The rod can be held. Bites can be felt and line paid out as required, but legering is often a little slow, and most anglers use rod rests.

Put the rod in the rest. Bites are registered by the twitching of the rod tip, but as this means constant watching, other indicators have been evolved.

When the fish gives a bite, take up the rod, engage the bale, hold the line momentarily against the spool with the forefinger, and strike. The force of the strike depends on the size of the fish sought, the strength of the tackle and the length of line out. A slight lift of the rod tip is sufficient if you are using light tackle and fishing fairly close in. If a fish takes a bait in 20 ft of water 40 yards out you will need to sweep the rod well back in order to take up the slack, overcome the elasticity of the line, and still drive the hook home.

It is possible to wander around with leger tackle fishing in

Legering in winter: in cold water fish tend to stay close to the bottom, and once the winter frosts have made weed growth die away there is less risk of a legered bait being hidden than there is in summer.

any likely deep hole, as described under float fishing, but the leger has no advantages over the paternoster (see below) which is generally better for this type of fishing.

Float Legering

Many anglers fish the leger with a float. The arrangement of the end tackle is the same, but a float is put on the line so that it shows on the surface when the leger weight is on the bottom.

The float indicates bites readily and makes striking more effective, since the line from rod to float is on the surface instead of being sunk to the leger weight.

On the other hand you can fish only in water no deeper than the length of the rod (unless you introduce the added complication of a sliding float) and ordinary float fishing or laying-on is usually just as good in those circumstances.

I do not recommend this method, but if you try it, put

enough shot on the line just below the float to sink the float to its tip, thus reducing its buoyancy and the resistance it offers to a taking fish.

Paternoster Fishing

In paternostering a weight heavy enough to hold the bottom is tied to the extreme end of the line. A hook on a hook-length is then attached to the line at any desired point to a loop (*Figure 16*) or a three-way swivel.

It will be seen that by this method a bait can be fished at any height above the bottom. In practice it is not usual to fish baits more than a few inches off the bottom.

The main reasons for the method are: (1) to fish for species such as perch that frequently take suspended baits, (2) to keep the bait above the debris of a pond or other water with a foul bottom, (3) to keep a bait above or among the upper fronds of dense weed, (4) to fish deep and distant waters.

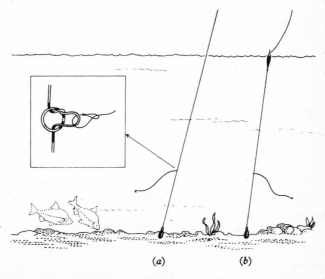

(*a*)   (*b*)

Figure 16   (a) *Paternoster.* (b) *Float paternoster.* **Detail drawing:** *attaching the hook-length to the main line.*

61

It will be seen from *Figure 16(a)* that if you are using a pater-noster close under the rod top the line will be almost vertical. If you are fishing 30 yards out the line will be at a low angle and the hook-length will have to be tied on higher up the line in order to keep the bait off the bottom.

Any sort of weight will do for paternoster fishing, though pear-shaped ones are perhaps best.

In ordinary paternoster fishing follow the rules for detecting bites, etc. mentioned under leger fishing.

Float Paternoster. *Figure 16(b)* shows the arrangement of a float paternoster. The float supports the line between weight and float, doing away with the acute angled line. The remainder of the line floats on the water and makes striking easier. Floats other than sliding floats cannot be used if the depth of the water is greater than the length of the rod.

Wandering with the Paternoster. With floatless paternoster tackle fitted up you wander from point to point, lowering or swinging the bait into gaps in the weed, testing the deep water by the lock gates, and, in winter, casting to the deeper water, or into known holes where fish of several species are likely to con-gregate, and into quiet backwaters when a river is in flood.

CHAPTER 5

Poles and Whips

The biggest revolution in angling over the past 30 years has to be the roach pole. Its title is slightly misleading as many species can be caught with the pole, although it was originally designed for catching roach. Using a pole is probably the easiest method of getting a beginner to catch fish. But the whole world of poles and ways of using them is a science in itself, and would need much more than this book to cover the subject in detail.

The beauty of poles is that you can present a bait with lightness and complete accuracy, and it's a method which encompasses waggler and stick float tactics all in one. Also available are whips which are really just small poles. The major difference is you don't use elastic and this limits them to taking small fish close in. Your rig is joined to a whip by looping it around the end, and it is secured by two lengths of silicone tubing. This chapter is just a brief introduction to the method and its associated bits and pieces.

The Pole

Nearly all modern poles are made from carbon or graphite composites, and come in lengths from as little as 3 metres to as much as 18 metres.

They come in sections which fit inside each other for storage, with everything fitting into the butt section. Buying a pole can be a daunting prospect as there are so many on the market, but the main thing to remember is always buy the best and longest you can afford. The most expensive poles can reach astronomical prices, some as much as £8,000, but the average pleasure angler will obviously be paying much less. Many good quality poles can be bought for around £250. You may be able to buy one secondhand for a lot less. The aim is to get the stiffest

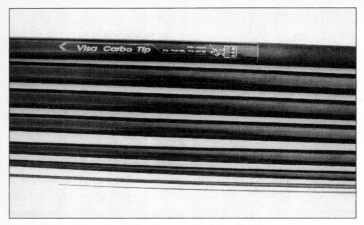

A modern carbon pole broken down to its individual sections.

pole you can, while ensuring the stiffness still remains along as much of the pole as possible. Another factor is how light the pole is – after all you have to be comfortable when holding 11 or more metres for a few hours!

Poles rely on special elastic fitted inside the top sections to absorb the lunges of a fighting fish. Once the fish is ready to be landed the sections can be taken apart and the fish brought closer to the net. This process is known as unshipping, and requires plenty of practice to master. The elastics come in various thicknesses to cope with different sizes of fish. Size 2 elastic will cope with light workloads, say canals and small river fish. A step up to size 5 or 6 will manage larger river species such as tench and bream. The many carp pools around the country stock fish of 10 lb or more and will require strong stuff in the region of size 13 or 14. All elastics should be lubricated before every session, with special liquid available from tackle shops.

Rigging your Pole

The items needed to complete your pole are firstly a Stonfo connector, which acts as the link between the elastic and your rig line. You also need a bung, which fits inside the pole sections and anchors the elastic. Some bungs can be adjusted to give varying tension. The final part is the bush which fits into the end of the pole to allow smooth running of the elastic, and a firm base for the Stonfo connector.

If you are unfamiliar with poles and their workings it's best to ask your local tackle dealer to explain it to you. Most will be more than happy to show you how to use them and some will even rig them for you.

Rigs

The joy of pole fishing is in its simplicity, and this is testified by the use of ready-made float rigs, kept on plastic holders called winders. Many an hour can be spent making these at home. There is a tool to allow you to shot the floats correctly in a bucket of water. This is called a neutral-density shotter and can be bought from the tackle shop. Normal split shot can be used, or there is another style of weight called the styl. These are elongated weights which come in handy if you are fishing with hempseed as bait. The fish will not confuse them with the shot, which are round and often mistaken for seeds by the fish. Also available is the olivette weight, which can be used instead of a bulk of separate split shot. You will be amazed at the thousands of different pole floats available, but the novice need only concentrate on two patterns. The first is known as body-up and is used for rivers with flow. Its upside-down pear shape is used for holding back when trotting through the swim. Still water fishing means you have no flow, so a body-down float is needed. The whole rig is fastened to the winder using a device called an anchor, and these are made of rubber or plastic.

The pole rig is kept on the winder until you start fishing. When you are ready, fix the end of the rig to the Stonfo connector, and unwind the rig from the winder. The first task will be to plumb the depth as with ordinary float fishing and this is explained elsewhere in this book.

As for the rest, a separate book would be needed to explain the various methods, as there are so many of them. I suggest you

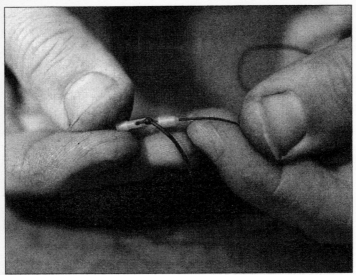

The Stonfo connector being attached to elastic (▲), and the bung to anchor the elastic inside the pole (▼).

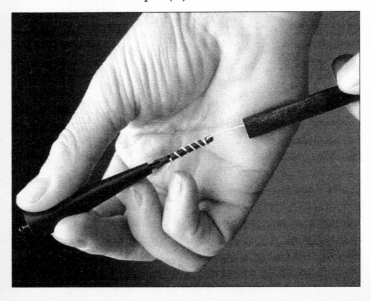

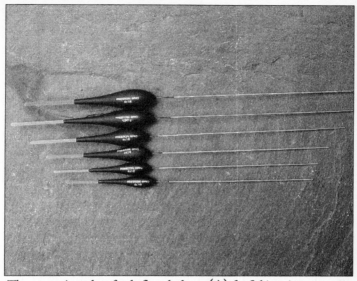

The two main styles of pole float: body-up (▲) for fishing rivers or any waters with flow, and body-down, for stillwater fishing (▼).

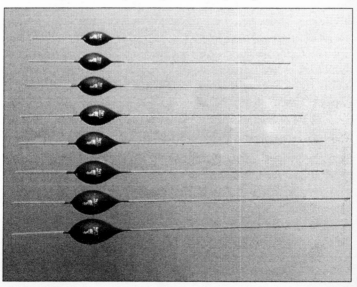

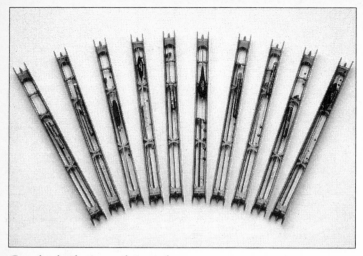

Completed pole rigs on their winders.

buy one of the many titles available as this will give you a much better grounding. If you do decide to take up pole fishing you will find it a brilliant method. Most match anglers own a pole, and many pleasure anglers are taking up the method, as a wide range of species can be caught with them. The best place to start is your tackle dealer as he can give you plenty of advice on which poles are suitable. Ideally, you would buy one or several of the many angling magazines available, who all publish articles on pole fishing. It can be a deadly method on the right day, but can take a while to master – once you've picked one up, it's unlikely you'll want to put it down!

CHAPTER 6

Baits and Groundbaits

Coarse fish are irregular feeders. At times some of them may be ravenously hungry; at others they will not feed at all, and most species are capable of going without food for many days. Between those extremes there are all sorts of conditions – times, for example, when one or two species are feeding and the rest are 'off'; times when they will take one bait and ignore half a dozen others; and times when they can be tempted to feed by a judicious offering of groundbait.

Except in the first condition, when the fish will take almost anything edible, bait is of supreme importance, and the choice of bait and its presentation makes the difference between success and failure.

Coarse fish have been caught on almost countless baits, some of them seasonal, some reasonably good and worth a trial, some merely freakish and not worth bothering about.

There are, however, three groups of standard baits, one or more of which are useful for all species of coarse fish at all times. These are maggots, bread and worms. I shall deal with these three groups at some length, and refer briefly to the remainder.

Maggots

Maggots are the grubs of the bluebottle. The grubs of similar flies have been named by anglers 'specials', 'squats', etc., but these are not important to the beginner.

The essential creatures are ordinary maggots. They *can* be bred at home but I strongly advise you to buy your maggots from the tackle dealer.

Maggots can be bought in their natural white colour, or dyed bronze, red, yellow and even green!

The demand for maggots is such that the supply is no longer in the hands of a few men who bred maggots in the backyard. Large and scientifically organised establishments now breed maggots by the million and send them out in bulk to tackle dealers, and by the pint or more to individual buyers. If you have any difficulty in getting maggots locally you will find plenty of advertisements in the angling press.

You will find your first maggots a mass of wriggling grubs, pointed at one end (the head) and thick and blunt at the other.

Sort these through before setting out to fish and put the largest and most vigorous specimens into one container, for hook baits, and the remainder into another for use as groundbait.

You will come across anglers using coloured maggots. The colouring is achieved in the feeding process or, later, by external dyeing. This is a refinement which can be forgotten until you gain experience.

Maggots are not a bait for pike. Perch have been caught on them but a worm is a better bait. *All other species of coarse fish*, if they are feeding at all, are likely to take maggots at any time or season. They are the top bait for roach and rudd and very good for bream and chub.

Hooking

Maggots, like caterpillars, seem to contain nothing but fluid. If your hook penetrates deeply into the body this liquid will escape, leaving a useless piece of skin on the hook.

Hook the maggot just through the skin at the blunt end (*Figure 17*). One maggot on a small hook is usually sufficient for roach and rudd, but two, three or four can be used on larger hooks for bream and chub and for general fishing when the water is coloured. No matter how many you put on they should all be hooked in the same way, lightly through the skin.

Hooks size 12 down to the smallest are suitable for single maggots. Sizes 8 and 10 can be used for bunches of maggots.

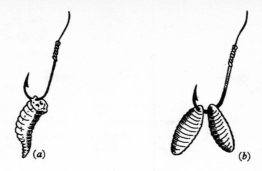

Figure 17 (a) *The best way to hook a maggot.* (b) *The chrysalis (often called a caster) into which a maggot develops also makes a good bait, used singly or two or three at a time. Hook them as lightly as possible, like maggots.*

Bread

Under this heading I include bread itself and paste made from bread and flour. In all their forms these baits are excellent for roach, chub, bream, dace, rudd, carp and tench.

Crust

Cut the bottom off a white loaf, just (and only just) removing the white part. This leaves a flat slab, varying in thickness according to the type of loaf from ¼ in to ⅜ in, consisting of the dark brown outer crust and the inner crust paling off from brown to fawn.

Crust is used in cubes or in irregular pieces. To make cubes, cut some of the crust into strips ¼ in to ½ in wide and then into pieces of various sizes up to ½ in long.

They can be conveniently carried in a tin.

Always take with you an uncut piece of crust. If the fish are disinterested, or suspicious of carefully cut shapes, they may be tempted by an irregular piece of bread simply torn roughly off the crust.

Hook sizes 10 and 12 are suitable for small pieces of crust. The large sizes (for carp and tench) can be used on sizes 6 and 8.

Figure 18   Three kinds of bread bait. (a) Crust: work the hook in from the soft side and push the point right through the crust. (b) Flake: lay the hook on a piece of flake, fold some of the flake over the eye and shank of the hook and pinch it firmly. (c) Mould paste onto the hook. Paste should not be too stiff – just firm enough to stay on the hook when casting.

The hook can be worked into the cube, but the point should be forced out through the crust, so that it is free to hook a fish at the slightest touch.

Flake

Opinions differ about the exact definition of flake, but it is generally regarded as a pinch of bread from the soft part of a white or brown loaf. It is at times a killing bait, but it is difficult to keep on the hook and can only be used, therefore, when the fishing needs no more than a gentle swing.

Some anglers use the soft part of the loaf with a little of the inner crust attached, the latter giving a firmer hook-hold than does the bread alone. Hook sizes 8 to 12.

Bread Paste

Cut three or four ½ in thick slices from a white loaf at least a day old. Trim off the crusts and wrap the slices in a cloth. Soak the bundle in water, squeeze out the surplus moisture and (still through the cloth) knead the wet bread with the fingers until it forms a firm paste.

Soak the break in rain-water or at the waterside. It is possible that chemicals in some tap water will flavour the bait unpleasantly.

A lump of paste is moulded round the hook, leaving the point free. Hook sizes 6 to the smallest, according to the quarry.

Flour Paste

Add water gradually to plain or self-raising white flour until a firm paste is obtained. A lump the size of a cricket ball is enough for an average day's fishing. Use in the same way as bread paste.

Liquidised Bread

This can be a brilliant method for roach and chub. Cut some slices of bread into strips and then cubes, then place in a liquidiser. The light, fluffy grains can be put in a swimfeeder and a pinch of flake placed on the hook. On its own it can be a very effective loose feed.

Flavourings

I have deliberately specified white bread and flour, because the whiteness itself is an attraction to most fish, but carp and tench have shown a liking for brown bread and paste.

Various flavourings, scents and colourings can be added to pastes but those are matters for experiment when you have gained general experience.

Worms

For angling purposes worms can be divided into four categories – lobworms, red worms, brandlings and others. In the last group are such creatures as marsh worms, gilt-tails, and what can be best called garden worms, i.e. the various worms found when digging, most of which, I believe, are lobworms in early stages of development.

I shall say something about them, but do not worry much about species of worms at this stage. *Any* worm is a good bait.

Lobworms

These are the long reddish worms with slightly flattened tails that emerge – or partially emerge – in darkness on damp lawns and grasslands. They are also encountered in ordinary garden digging. They are anything from 4 in to 10 in long.

I think they are very good baits for barbel and large perch; and they are very good indeed for carp, tench and eels. Many large bream have been caught on them. It is only their size that prevents smaller species of fish from taking them and it is an established practice to use the tail end of a lobworm for roach and dace fishing when rivers are in flood. Much though I value lobworms as bait, I must say that in my experience I have never found the tail of a lob to have any advantage over a smaller whole worm.

Lobworm collecting has been raised almost to the status of big game hunting and many thousands of words have been written on the subject. Essentially it means going out in soft-soled shoes after dark on to grassland, armed with a torch and a tin. The torch shows up the worms. Usually they still have a portion of their tails in the hole and withdraw completely if they hear heavy footfalls. When within reach of a lobworm, bend quickly and seize the exposed portion. Do not pull. Hold it between finger and thumb for about 15 seconds and you can withdraw it easily.

I now collect all lobworms I come across in normal garden work and keep them in a worm box (described later). This gives me more than an ample supply without resorting to cloak-and-torchlight methods.

The third method is to buy them. Many advertisers in the angling press send out any required quantity of lobworms, red worms or brandlings. You can also buy them in most tackle shops.

Hooking. About a quarter of its length from the head of a lobworm there is a raised band. Put the hook once through the body a little behind this band. This is sufficient for occasions when long casting is unnecessary and when 4 in to 6 in worms are being used. If you withdraw a worm like this from the water

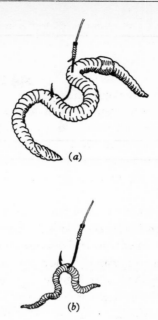

Figure 19   (a) *Baiting with a lobworm: pass the hook twice through the bait, leaving the ends free to wriggle.* (b) *Hook a brandling or small red worm just once through its middle.*

you have been fishing for five minutes it will hang down motionless on each side of the hook and look completely useless. Lower it into a few inches of water at your feet and you will see how active it immediately becomes.

If the cast demands more than a simple swing you may jerk the worm off the hook. In these circumstances pass the hook through twice, as shown in *Figure 19*. This method is also advisable for larger worms.

Hook sizes 6 or 8 for large worms and fish like barbel, carp, tench and large perch. Size 10 for smaller worms.

Red Worms

The active, bright red worms are usually 2 in to 3 in long. They are ideal baits for gudgeon, dace, rudd and perch, and, of course, may always be taken by bigger worm-eating fish. Hook sizes 10 downwards.

Brandlings

These are another species of small worms, usually found in well-rotted manure. They have distinct yellow bands and an odour detectable even by human beings. It is probable that many fish have a highly developed sense of smell and it is claimed that the brandling's scent is a factor in its favour as bait. Hook sizes 10 downwards.

Worm Boxes

Lobworms, red worms and garden worms can be kept for long periods in a wooden box. If you have a garden, half sink the box in the soil. If not, stand it on a doubled sack.

Half fill it with earth or leaf mould. Put in the worms, throwing away any damaged ones. Keep the soil moist (but not running with water), add a handful of half-rotted leaves once a week, or a similar quantity of dry tea leaves *after* tea has been made from them.

Keep the box covered (especially at night) with a sack. In long spells of dry weather keep the sack moist.

Protect the box from frost by earthing up the sides (in a garden) or, elsewhere, by wrapping in sacking.

Other Baits

In your first season's fishing the baits already mentioned should be sufficient, for you will almost certainly catch fish of several species with them and you will be too busy perfecting the manipulation of your tackle to have much time for experiment. However, I add here a short list of other baits that have proved useful.

Bloodworms. These are the thin, dark-red wriggling creatures that are to be seen in old water butts. They are actually the larvae of various gnats, and they are eaten by the million by such fish as carp, tench and gudgeon. I think every coarse fish except a pike could be tempted with bloodworms, but the trouble is they are small, very frail, and difficult to put on the hook. They are worth an experiment if you are endowed with patience and deft fingers.

One thing to remember with bloodworm is that it is banned on many waters. Check with your local club or fishery owner first before using them. Hook sizes 16 or 18.

Cheese. Any sort of cheese cut into small cubes or solid rectangles is a very good chub bait at all times. Processed cheese can be moulded on to the hook like paste. Blue cheese, with its very strong scent, can be a fantastic bait for big chub.

Sweetcorn. Bought in tins from the supermarket, this can be excellent for tench, carp and bream, although other species have been known to fall for it.

Fish. Small, dead freshwater fish are baits for pike, perch and eels. They are allowed to lie on the bottom. Hooks sizes 4 to 8 can be used according to the size of the bait. Very small fish – 3 in and less – can be hooked through the lips. With larger baits put the hook through the mouth and out at the gills, and then, to secure it in position, pass it once through the pectoral fin.

Live fish (livebait) are used as bait for predatory fish such as pike, perch and chub. Not all waters allow livebaiting, either to protect fish stocks or for ethical reasons – sometimes both. Don't forget, check first if it's allowed.

Slugs. These are mostly taken by chub and the best method is often to freeline them (no weights or float, just the hook).

Hempseed. You may hear a lot about hempseed as bait. It is very good in some waters in certain conditions, but its use is forbidden in others. It is prepared like wheat, but is a bait that can well be neglected until you have gained general experience.

Potatoes. Small half-boiled potatoes are a recognised carp bait.

Figure 20   When baiting with stewed hemp or wheat, simply push the bend of the hook into the soft core of the grain, where the skin has split.

Wasp grubs. Wasp grubs in the stage jut before their wings are defined will often tempt roach, rudd and dace particularly, and other species with less certainty. If you hear of a wasps' nest being 'treated' arrange to get some of the comb complete with grubs. They can sometimes be bought from bait dealers.

Wheat. A roach bait. The wheat should be simmered until the skin just splits to show the white kernel. Use on hooks 14 or 16.

Groundbait

In reasonable weather an angler who goes to the river, canal or pond and uses suitable tackle, methods and bait stands a good chance of catching a few fish, but to ensure continued success in coarse fishing, groundbaiting is essential.

I said 'to ensure' – but nothing in angling is certain. It would be better to say that when fishing for most of the coarse fish by accepted methods, groundbaiting multiplies your chances of success.

Groundbaiting has become almost a fine art, especially to the match fisherman, and you can buy gadgets that open on the river bed to release groundbait near your hook, and funnelled tubes through which liquid groundbait can be poured. There is no need to bother with such contraptions at this (or possibly any other) stage in your angling career. I mention them only to emphasise the importance accorded the subject.

Reasons for Groundbaiting

The reasons for groundbaiting and the ways of administering groundbait differ with the species and the character of the water.

Fish like pike and perch that pursue live prey hunt by sight more than smell, and groundbait is rarely used for them.

In most of the other coarse fish the sense of smell is highly developed and groundbait attracts and holds them. Those are the twin objects – attraction and retention – and holding them entails constant small contributions of groundbait all the time fishing goes on.

At the same time the groundbait must never fill them up. It is intended to stimulate appetite and not to satisfy it.

In these days of intensive fishing there is another important point. If you are lucky enough to be able to fish in private water or a stretch of river little visited by anglers you *may* catch fish without using groundbait, but most anglers have to fish on fairly crowded water. If you are fishing, let us say, in a canal with an angler on each side of you 20 or 30 yards away, it is almost certain that they will both be using groundbait. If you do not do so you will weight yourself out of the race. The odd fish may find your bait but the majority will remain in the vicinity of the groundbaited areas.

It may be thought that I am being too insistent on this subject. Let me put it in its proper proportion. If all you require of angling is a day in the fresh air, freedom from care, and an occasional fish, you can forget about groundbait. If you find that your greatest pleasure in angling comes from catching a lot of fish you *must* use groundbait.

Cloud Groundbait

This is the bait normally used in still water or waters with only a negligible current.

Basically it is breadcrumbs reduced to almost dust-sized particles. When it is moistened it can be shaped into a ball that will hold together long enough to be thrown to the float. The moment it touches the water it disintegrates, and the particles spread and sink very slowly. This clouds the water, attracting the fish and screening the angler and his movements from their sight.

It becomes a centre of attraction. There is no substance in it, but it creates a sense and smell of food. Small fish will investigate. Their movements probably set up fish radar waves which are picked up by better fish. When these arrive they are likely to remain in the area until the water clears. The angler keeps it cloudy by repeated doses of groundbait.

All tackle dealers sell groundbait in various sized bags. The easiest and cheapest for the novice is basic brown crumb. This is mixed to varying degrees with water, then left to stand for a few minutes to soak up the moisture. Then go back and add more water if needed. You can buy many other types of groundbait made by various manufacturers, which come in a multitude of flavours and smells. These can be expensive to the beginner and are probably left until you have more experience. A cost-effective method is to buy one bag of the flavoured stuff, and mix it with ordinary brown crumb. You can enhance the effect of groundbait by adding such loosefeed as maggots, corn, hempseed and worm, depending on the species you are seeking. Groundbaiting is a very wide subject and many top match anglers spend a great deal of time studying it. The beginner can wait until they are further down their angling career before involving themselves any deeper than the basics.

Bread Groundbait

Cloud groundbait is ideal because it cannot satisfy however much it may attract.

Unfortunately it can be used successfully only in still or nearly still water. Even a very moderate current washes it downstream. It is necessary to have something heavier in rivers.

The simplest form of river groundbait is made by soaking bread in water, wrapping it in a cloth, squeezing out the water and kneading it. The bread should be two days old or more, but not mouldy. One whole loaf should suffice for five or six hours' fishing.

This groundbait breaks up when it reaches the bottom. It provides actual food in small particles and should therefore be used sparingly. It can be lightened and made more firm by the addition of bran.

At the riverside, before finally adjusting your tackle, you will find out the depth of your swim. You must then estimate how far upstream you should throw your ball of groundbait so that it will reach the river bed at the top (i.e., the upstream) end of your swim. This depends on depth and the speed of the current.

It is better to overestimate than underestimate this distance. If the groundbait travels down with the current beyond your swim it will not only be useless but definitely harmful, for it will draw fish away from you. (In this connection, always be careful where you throw any sort of groundbait. If it comes to rest outside your fishing range it will merely tend to keep fish out of your reach.)

Presuming the distance has been correctly estimated the ball of groundbait will be borne along by the current as it sinks until it reaches the river bed. There it breaks up into particles, some of which lodge in crevices and behind stones, while others drift further into your swim. Some lighter fragments will be borne downstream and these may well bring fish searching along the scent beam for the main supply.

A lump the size of a tennis ball will do to start with, followed by golf ball–sized lumps at about 20 minute intervals – unless you have gathered a shoal of feeding fish in the swim, when you can throw in a small ball every few minutes to keep them interested.

If you are using maggots, worms or paste as hook baits it is an advantage to add a very few small maggots, small worms or little pellets of paste to the balls of groundbait.

Different methods of fishing demand different groundbaiting techniques. These are described in the next chapter.

Baiting-up

This is the term used for groundbaiting some time before you fish. There are no fixed rules and it varies from baiting an area once or twice every 24 hours for several days to putting some groundbait overnight in the pitch you intend to fish in the morning.

In the first instance the idea is to accustom fish to finding food at one spot, so that they will make a habit of visiting it in their travels. It is particularly valuable in large lakes, where fish are usually difficult to find.

If you live close to a water that is not heavily fished baiting-up is a valuable aid. In recent years it has lost popularity mainly because the majority of anglers live a long way from the waters they fish; and because, owing to intensive fishing, it is highly probable that you will find your carefully baited pitch occupied by someone else when you arrive to gather the fruits of your labour.

Any system of baiting-up, including overnight baiting, is especially useful for barbel, bream, carp and tench fishing.

If you are to fish from the bank note *exactly* where you have placed the feed.

CHAPTER 7

Fish and
Their Habits

I propose to deal at some length with roach, bream, chub, perch, tench and eel, which are widely distributed. One or more of the species will be found in nearly every coarse fishing water.

Dace, carp, grayling, rudd and barbel get slightly less attention, as do three small species, bleak, gudgeon and ruffe. The two imported species, catfish and zander, are mentioned briefly. Pike are normally caught by specialist methods not covered in the previous chapters.

The identification of these species is best established by noting the overall shape of the fish and the number, shape and position of the fins. In distinguishing roach from rudd the shape of the underjaw is a useful guide.

The presence or absence of barbels (fleshy tentacles dangling from the mouth) are further external clues. Colour is an

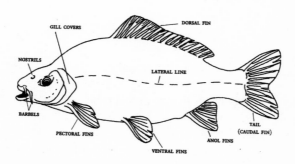

Figure 21   The principal features of a coarse fish.

unreliable guide, for it is subject to wide variation, and such colour schemes as I mention below are not intended as clues to identification.

Roach

People who do not fish and those who fish only for salmon, trout or pike wonder why coarse fish anglers put such a premium on roach. From their point of view the roach is a small species (it very rarely exceeds 3 lb in weight).

Many coarse fish anglers have become specialists of one sort or another, but most of them included roach fishing in their apprenticeship and they have no such doubts. Whatever other people may think about them, roach have captured the imagination of tens of thousands of anglers who would sooner catch a 2 lb roach than the biggest trout or barbel that swims. Scores of thousands of anglers fish expertly and happily for bream and other coarse fish when water and weather conditions demand it, but their main joy is roach fishing and they return to them as soon as they can.

I cannot give definite reasons for the popularity of roach. One concrete reason is that they are found in rivers, streams, lakes, ponds and pits in every part of the country from the south of Scotland southwards, so they are familiar fish to everyone who fishes coarse waters.

After that it is anybody's guess. Some anglers inherit an addiction to roach fishing. Some, in their apprenticeship, catch a few roach with comparative ease and go back to the same spot with the same bait in the same conditions – and never get a touch. That creates a challenge that must be met and in meeting it they become roach addicts.

The challenge is the main thing, and whether the fish be in a strong river or a semi-stagnant pond, they offer some problem. They feed at odd times in any combination of season, temperature and weather, and their choice of food can be most erratic. It is this uncertainty in behaviour, which often sends the most

A fine trio of prime, scale-perfect roach.

expert angler home without a touch, that makes the roach such an attractive antagonist.

Description

The roach has the normal coloration of most species of fish — dark on the back and upper sides in shades of brown, green and even deep blue in certain lights; silver on the sides and white on the belly. A notable characteristic is the red tinge on the fins. This is sometimes a brilliant scarlet, particularly in lower fins and the tail fin.

Note that the upper lip is thick and slightly protruding and that the dorsal fin is almost central on the back.

Size

The roach record is held by a fish weighing 4 lb 3 oz caught in the River Stour in Dorset in October 1990. The previous record was held by a roach caught in 1973 weighing 4 lb 1 oz. Many life-long roach fishermen have failed to catch a 2 lb roach – and anything above a pound is a good fish for the average run of waters.

Where to find Roach

In Rivers. Roach are not very fond of brilliant light and on sunny days they tend to feed in the shade and in deep swims.

They are particularly fond of swims over gravel or stone between beds of weed. They do not mind a reasonably strong current and it always pays to try a few runs down the main stream especially in times of drought. In cold weather they are inclined to seek deep water.

In flood conditions roach, like most other fish, seek shelter in deep holes, backwaters, eddies and the sheltered water below islands, jetties and similar formations.

In Canals. Roach may be anywhere. They tend to cruise up and down in a shoal and the water alongside a belt of reeds is a favourite spot. In very hot or very cold weather they may seek deeper water near lock gates.

In Lakes and Reservoirs. It is difficult to find where any sort of fish feed in big lakes and reservoirs and roach are no exception. Try anywhere except in the shallows, but until you get to know the water well it is best to rely on local advice.

Feeding Habits

When feeding, a shoal of roach is likely to cruise around in still water or move very slowly upstream in a river. At such times they are prepared to halt and mill around over any path of ground that contains or promises food. They take food at any depth and will take flies at the surface, but they do most of their feeding at or very close to the bottom.

Roach do not habitually eat other fishes, but with that exception they will take almost anything that is edible and of suitable size.

Although they are known to eat a wide variety of food they exercise bewildering changes of fancy, and the food or bait of today may be scorned tomorrow. There are, too, definite feeding periods, but when these start and end is unpredictable.

They do not seem to feed well on hot sultry days, or in waters holding quantities of dead leaves in the autumn; and they are subject to other fasting fits for which no reason can be given.

On very rare occasions roach take food ravenously, but generally they are dainty and suspicious feeders. Many of the roach waters are steadily fished by scores of anglers for nine months every year and the fishes' suspicions are justified. They are prepared to take into their mouths, or at least in their lips, anything that is not too obviously attached to a line, but they are also prepared to eject it with incredible speed. This habit has an important bearing on float watching and striking in roach fishing.

Fishing for Roach

In Rivers

Fishing the Swim. Fishing the swim is the standard method. Any form of roach fishing needs light tackle, but in a fairly strong current line of 3 lb is not too heavy. The bait will be moving quickly and the roach has no time to examine it closely. When you have hooked a roach it will have the force of the current to help its struggles and that puts an added strain on the line. When you gain experience you may elect to use finer terminal tackle, but until you do it is better to hook and land one fish than to hook and lose a dozen.

Bait with maggot, crust, flake or paste on hooks sizes 12 to 14. Once your groundbait starts to do its work, roach may gather in the swim.

To begin with, strike at *any* movement of the float, whether it be a dip, a lifting, a momentary halting, or even a tremble. Your bait should be tripping along the bottom and as it does so irregularities may affect the float, but until you learn to recognise these artificial influences, strike at once.

Striking does not mean a strong heave. In this type of fishing with only a few yards of line out, a twist of the wrist is sufficient. If you do not connect with a fish let the float run on to the end of the swim.

Long-trotting. This is an excellent method of fishing for roach in all waters that lend themselves to it.

Leger Fishing. Legering is a useful method for fishing deeps and weir pools and, in times of flood, the relatively slack water behind obstructions when long casting is required. A small worm is a good roach bait for legering when the water is highly coloured.

Still Water

Float Fishing. This method, which includes laying-on, is ideal for still shallow waters. The finest possible tackle is advisable when the water is clear. Use cloud groundbait and bait with a single maggot or a small pinch of bread flake on a 16 hook. A very sensitive variation of laying-on is to put one split shot 2 in from the hook. Gauge the depth exactly and adjust a very small float so that it lies at an angle of 45 degrees. The line is attached to the float only at the bottom end. This is extremely delicate tackle and the slightest touch on the bait registers on the float (*Figure 22*).

Leger Fishing. For still water roach fishing this method is especially useful in lakes and reservoirs where it is necessary to fish some distance from the bank; in deep water including that of pits; in stormy weather; and in the winter months.

Use the lightest leger weight consistent with your purpose.

Bronze (or Common) Bream

When coarse fish are judged by their popularity with anglers, bream come an easy second to roach. They are not as widely

This angler looks more than happy with a nice 4 lb-plus bream from the River Nene.

distributed as roach because they do not like even moderately fast running water or shallow water of any sort.

That still leaves them plenty of territory, and they are to be found in nearly all the deep muddy drains, ponds, lakes, broads, canals and slow-flowing rivers that are characteristic of low-lying country. They are prolific in the Fens and the Broads, and in fact, over the whole of East Anglia and Lincolnshire.

They are plentiful throughout the Central Plain and in the rivers and drains of Sedgemoor, and they subsist in many ponds and lakes (sometimes as a result of stocking) outside these areas. Wales is for practical purposes breamless. Many suitable waters in the south of Scotland such as Castle Loch hold very good bream, and the extensive plains of Ireland are ideally suited to them.

Description

Bream are deep in the body in proportion to their length and are relatively thin.

They are a dark metallic shade of grey-brown or bronze on the back which gradually lightens down the sides to give way to an off-white belly colour. The lower fins may have a greenish tinge. Small bream are much lighter and more silvery in colour. Adult male bream can be identified during spawning by lots of white dots called tubercles on, and around, the head area. They are covered with a thick layer of slime.

Size

The current bream record stands at 16 lb 9 oz, which was caught at a Southern syndicate water. There are stories of fish reaching 20 lb but one has yet to be seen alive. It is much more likely, however, to hook a smaller fish and any bream of 4 lb or more is considered to be a good one.

Where to find Bream

Bream like grubbing in the mud in deep water, and in canals and drains they are likely to feed in the middle, this normally being the deepest part. They may also be found where there are holes and depressions in the bed. In rivers they will also seek the deeper parts but those are not necessarily in the middle.

In lakes, ponds, reservoirs and pits they may be anywhere outside the shallows, though if the bottom varies in composition they will seek out the mud areas.

Although bream feed and spend much of their time at the bottom, they come to the surface at times and can be seen rolling about, dorsal fins and backs showing well above the water. They are not likely to be caught at this time.

Feeding Habits

Bream live in shoals, and all the fish in a shoal usually come on the feed together. They are not fussy eaters and once they start they will go on eating steadily for, perhaps, as long as two hours. When they stop they are unlikely to feed again for several hours.

The feeding periods may come at any time, but dusk, the

early hours of the night and the very early hours of the morning are likely times, with emphasis on the early morning. They will also feed in broad daylight and many good bream and bags of bream have been taken when the sun was high. Groundbaiting may induce them to start feeding.

They feed on practically all the animal food that can be nosed out of the mud – worms, larvae, freshwater snails, freshwater mussels, etc. – and a shoal of large bream will consume a surprising quantity of food. They may at times eat up all the available food and that may be one reason for the occasional migration of large shoals of bream for considerable distances.

Fishing for Bream

Picture bream in their favourite haunts. The time to catch them is when they are feeding, and at that time they will have their snouts down in the mud and their tails raised high.

They are unlikely to see any suspended bait and no matter which method you use, the place for the bait is right on the ground.

Groundbait

Irrespective of method, too, is the need for groundbaiting. Cloud groundbait is recommended for general purposes in the sort of water bream delight in, but these fish need something more solid. Up to 20 cricketball-sized lumps of crumb with some worms or maggots added (if those are to be your hook baits) can be thrown in. The size of water you are fishing will determine how much feed you throw in. A good rule is to start off light and then throw in more to hold them once you have the fish feeding.

Bait

Lobworms and lobworm tails, red worms, brandlings and any other sort of worm are ideal baits. So are maggots; and when the fish are not being coy a bunch of four or five is better than a single maggot. They like bread in all its forms. If you use crust, which tends to float, put a split shot close to the hook to keep it down.

Hook sizes depend on the bait. Numbers 8 and 10 are normal, but you can use a 6 with a lobworm and 12 if the fish are shy.

Methods

I am going to recommend only two methods for bream fishing, laying-on and legering. Others can be tried when you have caught a few bream.

Laying-on. This is the method to use when: (1) the water you are fishing is not deeper than the length of your rod, (2) the fishing point is within your float-casting capabilities. Adjust the float exactly and have the first shot not less than 2 ft from the hook.

When the bream takes the bait it has its head down. As it assumes a normal horizontal position it will lift the shot when the float, relieved of the weight, will lie flat or nearly so. Strike when the float starts to move along the surface. Strike, too, of course, if the float goes down and away. Some other species or a bream acting abnormally may have taken the bait.

Legering. This is a most useful method. Remember that bream like deep water: the very centre of canals and drains, and often distant spots in lakes, reservoirs, pits and pools. Legering overcomes both long casting and deep water.

Silver Bream

From an angler's point of view the silver (or white) bream is an uninteresting poor relation of the bronze bream, for it offers little sport and is a much smaller species. Mature silver bream can be as little as 8 oz in weight and the average is 12 oz to 1 lb.

They are generally silver in colour and can be confused with young bronze bream. The scales along the lateral line of silver bream number 44-48: those of a bronze bream 50-57.

Chub

Chub are exciting fish. They are strongly built, muscular fish and though difficult to hook they put up a most sporting fight once the hook has been driven home.

They like rivers with a strong or steady flow that also provide deep water, though the rivers need not be deep throughout. Chub are quite happy in those rivers where fairly deep pools alternate with shallow rapids. They have been introduced into some still waters and sluggish rivers but they do not settle down well in such conditions.

In the right sort of river they are to be found throughout England except the extreme south-west, in northern Scotland and east Wales. Chub are not native to Ireland.

Description

Chub are big-headed, big-mouthed fish with a weight of flesh well forward, always a sign of a good fighting species.

The back is a dark grey or brown tinged with green, the sides silvery with a yellow tint, and the belly white. The fins are touched with red, especially the lower ones which may be entirely red.

Size

Although chub reaching 10 lb are talked about by specialist anglers, not one has been caught. The best at present is an 8 lb 10 oz fish taken from the River Tees. Match anglers love small chub as they can build up a good weight. Most specimen anglers would call anything over 5 lb good fish.

Where to Find Chub

Chub live in groups of from 4 to 5 to a dozen or so. They choose a safe home and remain in or near it. That home is almost invariably a pool of deep water out of the main current where there is some form of shelter. Tree roots projecting into the water beneath the surface prove a likely haunt, and an undercut bank is favoured. A fallen tree hanging over the water with its branches submerged is also likely to attract chub. Where such ready-made shelters are scarce, chub are likely to lie close in to the bank under overhanging bushes and trees.

Feeding Habits

Chub feed in three clearly defined areas: (1) at or near the surface in the sheltered positions near the banks, close to their holes among the tree roots, (2) in gravelly swims in the main current, where they face upstream and take any food washed down to them, (3) close to the bottom in deep water. (1) applies mainly in warm weather, (3) in cold weather and (2) at any time.

In the first situation they seem to be basking in the sun-warmed surface waters, ready, however, to make a dash for any caterpillar or beetle that falls from the bushes or any fly that alights on the surface. Small frogs are taken and any fish small enough to be swallowed that come into the pool. They have a definite liking for fruit and have been known to take up positions under overhanging cherry and elderberry trees when the fruit is ripe.

When they move out into the current they are usually hungry and will take anything edible that comes along – fish, crustacean, insect, mollusc or vegetable matter.

In cold weather they are not likely to have such keen appetites but a tempting bait is rarely refused if put in the right place, and some of the biggest chub may be caught in these conditions.

Fishing for Chub

There is one rule for successful chub fishing that must never be violated – *keep out of sight*.

If you manage to do this you can make a good many mistakes and still catch chub.

If, on a warm afternoon you approach a known chub hole, you may be able to see these broad-backed fish cruising slowly around, occasionally rising to take an insect deliberately from the surface or spurring into rapid action if a rival fish tries to get the same morsel. You will see this scene only if you have approached the screening bushes with a soft tread that has not set up vibrations.

Any unusual movement or vibration will disturb them. They do not dash for safety. They sink slowly out of sight and you will have to wait a long time before they reappear.

You can see and study the reactions of these surfacing fish. You will not be able to see those feeding in the current or at rest in deep holes. They can, however, see or sense you if you approach them too closely or if your shadow or the shadow of your rod falls on the water anywhere near them.

It is clear that your fishing position must be as far away from the fish as your tackle permits. Long-trotting in some form or another is the obvious answer.

Long-trotting

Basking Chub. Let us suppose that you have seen a shoal of chub near the surface or that you think they are or ought to be in a certain spot.

Assemble your tackle well away from the bank. Use 4 lb b.s. line and a 4 or 5 in small peacock float. Tie on an eyed hook, say, no. 8 for medium worms, no. 10 for a bunch of maggots, crust or paste.

Do not put on any split shot and let the hook hang only 2 ft to 3 ft below the float.

Approach the bank with the utmost caution at least 20 yards above the chub. Once there, study the position and see if your float will have a clear run down to the fish. If there are obstacles, move carefully downstream until you have passed them. If this is likely to bring you within 7 or 8 yards of the shoal, kneel or even lie down.

When you are in position, drop the bait and the float quietly into the water under your extended rod-tip, and, giving line freely, let the current take the float downstream in the usual long-trotting method, retarding the float by momentarily checking the line from time to time so that the bait travels ahead of it.

Strike the moment the float disappears, raise the rod tip and try to draw the chub out of its position. At the moment of striking the chub will be surprised and off guard and you may be able to get it a yard to two towards you. These rough tactics must not be continued. Their aim is firstly to get the fish away from the bolt hole to which it would dive if it got a chance. The second is to let it fight the battle away from the rest of the fish. If you achieve this purpose you may be able to hook a second fish from the same shoal.

Once the shoal is disturbed, move on to the next chub spot.

It is clear that this sort of fishing can be done only when there are few people about and you can move freely.

Chub in the Swim. These are the fish that have moved out into the main stream, often into relatively shallow water, and remain almost stationary except for short dashes after food brought down by the current.

The ideal way of long-trotting for them is from a punt anchored athwart the current. They may not be there when you start fishing, but groundbait may attract them towards you.

If there are no boats or punts available, try to find some spit of land or bend in the river where the current will carry your float down the main stream.

Gauge the depth exactly and arrange matters so that your bait just trips along the bottom. You will need a buoyant float and enough shot to keep the bait well down.

Use 4 lb b.s. line, and hook numbers 6, 8, 10 or 12 according to the size of the bait.

Leger Fishing

This method is useful in cold weather and when lack of a boat or a suitable position on land makes long-trotting impossible.

Follow the instructions for leger fishing, and, when you have cast out, remain motionless behind cover or well back from the bank if there is none. Groundbait with balls of bread mixed with bits of hook bait – and wait patiently.

Again 4 lb b.s. line is about right. First try hook sizes 6 or 8 with big baits. If there is no response after an hour but some indication that chub are about, reduce both the size of the hooks and the baits.

Baits

In addition to the standard worms, maggots and bread, chub have been caught on an almost endless list of baits including scores of insects, green peas, cherries, elderberries, banana cubes and macaroni. Unless you want to experiment, keep to standard baits, but mix plenty of grated cheese with your paste when you use that bait.

For basking chub use a small red worm, a brandling, or two or three maggots.

Use slightly larger worms, a bunch of three to five maggots, or a hazelnut-sized piece of paste for chub in the swim.

For legering, try a lobworm, a bunch of maggots, or a walnut-sized lump of paste.

Perch

Perch are my favourites among the coarse fish, a statement that may be puzzling to the artists who regularly catch big shy roach and to carp addicts whose whole technique is opposed to that used in perch fishing.

There is undoubtedly some prejudice against perch among anglers. This is due, I think, to the frequent presence of hordes of insatiable small perch which cannot be frightened off and which attack the bait as soon as it touches the water. They spoil the fishing of anglers trying to catch other species.

Perch fishing is often less a case of finding the fish (the main problem in most angling) than of avoiding the small ones.

Perch are very widely distributed over the whole of the British Isles except the Scottish highlands. They thrive in small ponds and large lakes; in reservoirs, meres, pits, broads and canals; and in nearly every type of river except shallow and fast-flowing ones.

Description

The perch has a distinctly humped back from which rise two dorsal fins, the first composed of stiff sharp spines. The ventral fin has one and the anal two spines.

Perch vary a great deal in colour. The back is very dark, but may be shades of grey, green or brown. The sides also are sombre, giving way to a dull white belly. The ventral, anal and tail fins may be red or tinged with red. Five or more vertical black bars ornament the sides. These are generally more distinct on perch taken from weedy water.

Size

The record rod-caught perch weighed 5 lb 9 oz and was caught in a private lake in Kent in 1985. Several other fish weighing over 5 lb have been reported but catching one is very unlikely, though not impossible. A 3-pounder is a very good fish and 2-pounders are perch to be proud of.

They keep together in shoals, the size of the fish in any one shoal being about the same. A general rule is that the bigger the fish the smaller the shoal. This is understandable for as the years pass accident, anglers, pike, and death from natural causes thin them out until, when the 5 lb state is reached, such a fish may be the sole survivor of its group.

There will naturally be shoals of small and growing perch, but the huge congregations to which I referred earlier are usually composed of mature fish that are unlikely to grow any bigger because of scanty food supplies or some biological upset.

Where to Find Perch

Several centuries ago anglers were advised to fish for perch by bridges, quays, jetties, rocks, stranded boats and similar structures or formations. For the average run of perch that advice is true today, and to the list can be added canal locks and their approaches.

Other good points are along the edges of extensive reed beds.

They are likely to visit rocks and reed beds in extensive lakes but it is advisable to ask local anglers where the perch haunts are in such waters.

Big perch are less likely to be in the routine places; and in ponds, pits and reservoirs it is well to try for them in deep water well out from the banks.

In rivers they prefer spots sheltered from the main flow of the current. There are exceptions to this, as you may discover when you are long-trotting for chub, but test the normal haunts before experimenting.

Feeding Habits
Perch are daylight feeders.

They are predatory fish and even small perch will chase, seize and eat any fish of suitable size. This tendency increases as they grow and large perch in certain waters live mainly on other fish. In winter they pursue such prey actively. In summer they may lie in ambush among the weeds in which they are so well camouflaged by their coloration and black bars.

They will take food from the bottom but more often they find what they want as they cruise around, nosing into weed beds and sucking off the small creatures that live in them, or poking around the weed-covered surfaces of the places already mentioned.

Fishing for Perch

Float Fishing
This is probably the most popular method of fishing for perch and it is ideally suited to most canals and small ponds and to rivers where the depth is not much more than 8 ft.

In Still Water. In still water use a very small float, 3 lb b.s. line with a no. 8 or 10 hook-to-nylon a trifle finer. Adjust the float so that the bait is suspended about 6 in to 1 ft above the bottom or just above the top of any well-submerged weed growth. Put enough shot *close to the float* to cock it. The bait will then sink naturally. It is often taken by a perch as it does so.

If you have found a spot which perch visit in their feeding round you have only to wait. If you feel energetic you can wander around casting the bait into likely spots, providing you do not spoil the sport of any other angler.

In Rivers. The tackle already described will do for most forms of river fishing, though some shot will have to be put a foot or so from the hook to take the bait down. Look for places out of the main current or protected from it by obstructions.

Paternoster Fishing

This is a good perch fishing method in medium depths (say 8 ft to 14 ft) and distances up to about 15 yards. Beyond that distance there is such an angle on the line that legering is a better method.

Use 4 lb b.s. line with a hook-to-nylon looped to it so that it fishes about a foot off the bottom. Wandering with a paternoster (Chapter 4) is often most successful.

Leger Fishing

Leger fishing is a favoured method for perch and it is very useful for fishing far out in deep ponds, pits, lakes and reservoirs.

A 4 lb or 5 lb b.s. line can be used with a number 6 or 8 eyed hook. Some really big perch have been caught in this way.

Baits

A lively worm is the ideal bait for all these forms of fishing. Any sort of worm is likely to tempt perch, but it may be well to use 3 in or 4 in red ones in clear water float fishing. A really large lobworm on a no. 6 hook is suitable for leger fishing.

▲ *The common carp.*   ▼ *The rudd.*

▲ *The grayling.*   ▼ *The pike.*

▲ *The barbel.* ▼ *The European catfish (wels).*

▲ The zander.   ▼ The gudgeon.

Perch will take maggots, but worms are better. They are not interested in bread or paste. No groundbaiting is necessary.

Striking, Playing and Handling

A perch usually makes the float bob a couple of times and then takes it down and away. Strike the moment it goes under after the bobbing stops. You then stand a good chance of hooking the fish in the lips or mouth. If you delay too long it will gorge the bait and you will have to use a disgorger to recover the hook.

Once hooked, a perch will give you a hard fight. It will attempt to seek the shelter of weeds and will usually bore strongly downwards. Do not try to get it (or any other fish) to the surface before it is beaten. A fish splashing about on the surface puts a heavy strain on the line.

In order to take out the hook, pass your *wet* hand up the head and back so that the spiny fin lies flat. Grip the fish firmly by the fleshy part of the sides (not by the soft belly parts) and take out the hook.

Livebaiting and Spinning

These are good methods as described for pike but you will need a fine wire trace, not because a perch is likely to snap the line, but a pike might. There is no way of telling if a pike will take the bait, but if it does you will have a chance of landing it. There is no excuse for fishing so light that a pike breaks the line and has to swim around with hooks in its mouth.

Tench

You fish alone for tench, or at most with one or two quiet companions. Tench are creatures of the weed beds and though they bite readily at times they are unlikely to do so if there is movement and vibration on the bank.

They are found in many still waters and some rivers of the British Isles, but the distribution is patchy. Tench waters become scarcer the further north one goes from Yorkshire and they peter out altogether at about the Clyde-Forth line. In England and

Wales they are to be found in countless ponds, pits and stretches of canals to which they have been introduced, as well as in lakes and rivers which the species has inhabited for centuries.

Description

Tench are solid-bodied, rounded fish with plenty of flesh on their bones. A small barbel descends from the corner of the mouth on each side. When the sun shines on a freshly-caught tench glints of gold are revealed, but for the most part the tench are sombre-hued, almost black on the back with dark green sides merging into a tarnished silver colour on the belly. All the fins are black or the darkest of greens.

Size

Either tench are growing bigger or the strong but fine lines of nylon monofilament are making the capture of big tench easier. In 1882 a 7 lb tench was caught in a clay pit near Weston-super-Mare. This remained the record until 1928, though it was equalled by another in 1933. In 1948 a tench of 7 lb 6 oz was caught in a gravel pit near Chichester. Then in 1950 a 8½ lb fish was caught in Leicestershire and a tench weighing 9 lb 1 oz was caught in 1963 in Huntingdonshire. The current record is held by a fish weighing 14 lb 7 oz, from a private Hertfordshire pit.

The records are not so important as the fact that the average weight of tench taken by anglers is increasing, and 5-pounders are now not uncommon. However, you will find a 2 lb tench a very satisfactory fish.

Where to Find Tench

Tench like weeds and mud. Given these they do not seem to worry how small a pond may be or how shallow the water. They lead secluded lives, burrowing for food deep in the mud, sometimes sending up pin-sized tench bubbles as they do so, and sucking a variety of creatures from the aquatic plants among which they live.

Figure 22   The 'lift method' is an extra-sensitive variation of laying-on popular for tench fishing. A small float, attached by the bottom end only, is cocked by a single swan shot resting on the bottom and set only 1-2 in from the bait (a). When a fish takes the bait it lifts the shot off the bottom and the float lies flat (b). This is the signal to strike.

When feeding seriously they may leave the plantations of aquatic plants for some nearby patch of open mud, but they never stray far from shelter.

Except in small ponds they are not usually spread evenly throughout the water. A small group may live and move around in, perhaps, a 500-yard stretch of a canal, and there may be no more in either direction for a mile or more. Experience, observation, and local knowledge are the best keys to tench haunts.

There are a good many solitary tench, but it is impossible to lay down rules for finding them and if they are caught it is usually by accident.

In large and unknown sheets of water, try fishing close to the edge of the beds of aquatic plants, concentrating on patches of water lilies if there are any.

Some rivers – the Kennet, for example – are good tench waters, but I advise the beginner to keep to still water in his early endeavours at tench fishing.

Feeding Habits

Tench seem to feed by smell and touch more than by sight and their barbels no doubt play a considerable part in selecting food from the many things they turn up as they nose in the mud.

As with all bottom-grubbing fish, bloodworms must form a high proportion of the intake whenever they are present, and worms and all the smaller creatures that subsist in mud and on the lower parts of plants are also eaten.

Tench feed only when the water is warm. They may eat half-heartedly when the water temperature is about 55°F, but their appetites improve as the temperature rises above this figure. This means that tench are summer fish. During the winter they burrow into the mud and remain there until the spawning period arouses them. There are exceptions to all these statements but they are true in the main.

Tench will feed in the given temperature conditions at any period during the summer and autumn, but statistics show that a majority of notable tench are caught in the latter half of June and in July. This probably applies also to lesser tench for which no figures are available.

The best time to catch tench is without doubt the hours from the first hint of light in the sky to about 8 or 9 a.m. Next best are the twilight of evening and the first two hours of darkness. They are occasionally caught in broad daylight.

Fishing for Tench

Tench are usually hooked among or close to the weed beds in which they live. As soon as they feel the hook they dive for cover. Ultra-fine tackle is useless. A no. 6 or 8 eyed hook tied to 5 lb b.s. nylon is as light as you should go. Camouflaged nylon is helpful in tench fishing.

In still water a small float will suffice, for the bait must lie on the bottom and there is no weight to support. Laying-on and legering are two good methods. I often fish for tench with a small float set so that about a foot of line lies on the bottom without weight except for a split shot close to the float to cock it.

Preparations

Whenever possible bait-up for tench any time from a couple of days to a few hours before fishing. Choose some likely looking spot, preferably a clear patch of mud within a few yards of weed beds, and throw in several balls of groundbait.

In canals and small ponds there may not be any gap in the weeds of sufficient size to make fishing possible. In such circumstances, make your own fishing place by clearing a patch about 3 or 4 yards across with a narrow channel through the bankside growth through which you can bring a fish to the net. The weed clearing can be done with an iron rake-head attached to a length of rope. Throw this in and let it sink. Pull it slowly along the bottom and the teeth will drag up the plants by their roots. Repeat this until you have a clear area.

Quicker results are obtained with two rake-heads lashed back to back but this makes a heavy and cumbersome load and there is an even chance that the single head falls teeth downward.

The clearance can be made the night before you fish or earlier. If this is impossible, do it as soon as you reach the water. You will scare all the tench but they will come back, sometimes in as little as an hour. There is usually a chance of catching some other fish elsewhere while you are waiting.

Fishing

Whether it is a cleared patch or more open water throw in a couple of tennis ball-sized lumps of groundbait, bait up, cast in, put the rod in its rest, sit down, and wait. Do not throw in any more groundbait until you catch a tench. You may have to wait a long time, but avoid movement as much as possible.

If all goes well you may see the tell-tale bubbles approaching your bait, though tench will often appear without any obvious sign. After some preliminary trembles the float will go decisively away. Strike, and be prepared to play a strong antagonist. Get the feel of your fish and exert as much pressure as is safe to keep it from reaching the weeds. Hold the rod at an angle of about 45 degrees so that its whole length comes into play.

If your efforts fail and the tench gets into a weed bed, relax the pressure and let the line go slack. Point the rod straight at the fish and then gently pull the line by hand. This process, known as handlining, sometimes coaxes the fish out. Once it is in open water again bring the rod into play.

Baits

A big lobworm, two or three small worms, or a walnut-sized lump of paste are really good baits for tench. Some anglers think brown bread paste better than white, and some add sugar or honey to both. Tench have been caught on breadcrust, maggots, sweetcorn and several other baits.

Eels

It is very hard to remain unacquainted with eels. Anyone in doubt about their appearance and activities on the hook will receive practical lessons very soon after he starts fishing.

This is not the place to tell the entrancing story of the eel's life story. It must suffice to say that from eggs laid by mature eels in the vicinity of the Bermuda Islands hatch out larval forms quite unlike eels, which reach British shores three years later. They turn into elvers which ascend the rivers and these in turn quickly change into eels. They penetrate the streams and ditches and make cross-country journeys to enclosed ponds until there are very few waters indeed without a quota of the year's eel arrivals. Every autumn a proportion of the male and female eels that have spent several years in fresh water go down the rivers and across the Atlantic to the breeding-place, where they spawn and die.

Figure 23   The eel.

Size

Many very heavy eels have been reported. Some were found dead and some caught on night lines or in nets and traps. The record is held by an eel weighing 11 lb 2 oz which was caught in 1978 in Kingfisher Lake, near Ringwood in Hampshire, so catching one of 7, 8 or even 9 lb is possible.

An eel of anything near that weight is very powerful, far more so than a normally shaped fish of the same weight, and powerful tackle is necessary to cope with them.

For every one such eel there are tens of thousands of others, ranging from 'bootlaces' a few inches long to one- and two-pounders.

Where to Find Eels

It is easy to find eels, and if you are fishing with worms, maggots or other fleshy baits the eels will do their best to find you. Skinny eels only a few inches long can be an insufferable nuisance on occasions, repeatedly taking the bait and coiling themselves into a slimy knot around the line when brought ashore. Bigger eels are easier to deal with but they can be disastrous if you are fishing very fine for shy fish.

Deliberate eel fishing is good sport. In canals, lakes and rivers they may be anywhere, but they like holes and cracks and they can usually be found near walls, locks, areas of broken rock, piers, piles and jetties. Though they subsist in swift strong streams they are much more numerous in still or slow-moving waters with plentiful mud.

Feeding Habits

The natural history books tell you that eels leave their hiding-places and move around in search of food during the hours of darkness. That is true of probably the majority of eels, but plenty move around and feed in the daytime, and this is especially true of the smaller specimens.

They eat almost anything fleshy, dead or alive, from the smallest of larvae to the biggest fish their elastic jaws can encompass. They catch and eat live fish, especially at night when their sight seems better than in daylight, and they also smell out and consume any fish corpses that lie on the bottom.

Like tench, they are warm-water feeders. They will feed at temperatures of 50°F or over, but water cooler than this puts them off, and in winter most eels retire into the mud and eat nothing until the spring.

Fishing for Eels

When you deliberately set out to catch eels you must forget most of the rules that govern ordinary fishing. Tackle must be strong, and there is no question of playing an eel gently: it must be brought to land as quickly as possible.

Tackle

I advise you not to fish for big eels unless you have a second rod much stronger than the ordinary bottom rod. You cannot, of course, be certain that you will not hook a really big eel when you go eel fishing but you can exercise some measure of control on the prospective size of your captures. If you fish in daylight with a worm bait you reduce the chances of hooking a monster.

The best places to fish are in still waters or very sluggish drains and rivers. There *are* eels in faster waters but captures will probably be few and small.

In narrow waters, such as canals, use a small float. In wide or deep water use leger tackle. In both cases a line of about 8 lb b.s. and a no. 6 hook tied direct to the end of the line will be suitable.

Bait

In daylight I believe eels feed more by scent than sight, and some forms of groundbait will attract them from considerable distances. Kipper, fresh liver, or bloody meat cut small are good attractors. The eels get an attractive smell and a hint of blood but no solid food.

For the hook bait I find a large lobworm as good as any.

Dealing with Eels

The float gives a series of quick bobs when an eel toys with the bait, and there may be a pause and a period of stillness before the bobbing starts again. Wait until the float moves off definitely and then strike.

As soon as you feel the fish, reel in as quickly as possible without pause. Drag the eel up the bank on to level ground and put the sole of your shoe on it an inch or two behind the head. Keep the line taut. You should then be able to remove the hook with your disgorger.

Big Eels

If you decide to try for big eels, fish in the evening twilight and the first hours of darkness, using a strong rod, a 12 lb b.s. line, a wire trace, a leger weight and a no. 4 hook baited with a small fresh fish such as a roach or gudgeon.

Keep the rod in your hands or hold the line near the reel so that bites can be felt. Then wait a few seconds before striking to let the eel get the bait well into its mouth.

Dace

Dace are silvery fish that delight in the clear waters of fast or moderately fast rivers. On bright or warm days they feed in the surface layers but on other occasions and in winter they are likely to be found near the bottom.

They are a relatively small species, the official rod-caught record currently standing at 1 lb 4 oz 4 drams. This fish was taken from the Little Ouse in 1960. A one-pound dace is a notable fish and the average, of course, is a matter only of ounces.

Dace are very like chub in build and colour, so much so that small chub are often thought to be big dace. There are several points of difference, but one that serves for rough and ready indentification is that the outer edge of the anal fin of a chub is convex while that of a dace is concave. (See colour plates.)

When dace are in surface waters they can be caught on the finest of tackle by suspending a no. 14 or 16 hook, baited with a single maggot or a small piece of bread or paste, about two feet beneath a 3 in float. Let this float down the swim. No ground-baiting is necessary. Dace eject a suspicious mouthful almost instantaneously and very quick striking is necessary.

When dace are feeding near the bottom the methods and baits used for roach are suitable.

Long-trotting is an excellent method and many dace are caught by anglers long-trotting for chub, especially when the float is halted at the end of its run and the bait rises in the water.

In spite of their small size dace put up a good fight.

Carp

There are three varieties of carp in British waters – the fully-scaled common carp, the mirror carp which has an incomplete row or two of large scales, and the scaleless leather carp.

They are well distributed in England and are to be found in southern Scotland. They are scarce in Ireland and Wales. They subsist in several of the bigger rivers but attain their best growth in ponds and lakes where there is a plentitude of food and a limited number of fish. It was in such a pond – Redmire Pool in Hertfordshire – that the record 51 lb 8 oz carp was caught in 1980. The current record stands at 55 lb 10oz and was caught at

Wraysbury. There are countless ponds containing so many carp that few ever attain a worthwhile weight.

But there are now many lakes in the country which are specially stocked with very big carp, some up to 40 lb, and which are very expensive to fish. These waters require methods far beyond the beginner and are best looked at when you have plenty of experience.

Fishing is at its best during the summer, though some good carp are often caught in the autumn. In recent years some dedicated anglers have been successful fishing at night in the depths of winter but as a general rule carp seem to stop feeding and go to ground during the winter and, like tench and eels, are generally disinclined to feed unless the water is warm.

The tackle and methods recommended for tench will prove adequate for carp of less than 10 lb. Fishing for the bigger carp is a job for which special tackle and preparation are necessary. It therefore lies outside the scope of this book.

Good sport may be had in the many ponds that hold smaller carp without elaborate preparation. Baiting–up is desirable but not essential, as is an initial offering of groundbait, but once you start to fish nothing should disturb the surface of the water and the angler should keep himself well hidden.

In addition to the methods and techniques already suggested for tench, carp will sometimes take a floating crust. No float or weight is used, and it is important to grease your line. Tear off a piece of crust from the side of a loaf leaving some of the white interior part of the loaf attached, so that the overall size and shape is roughly that of a match-box. This should be attached to no. 4 hook and gently cast out to where the carp have been feeding. If you need to cast a long way you can make the crust heavier and easier to cast by dipping it momentarily in the water first. However, if there is a breeze it may be possible to make the crust drift for the last part of its journey, which will reduce the risk of frightening the fish. A few loose pieces of crust can be thrown in around the hooked crust to act as attractor bait.

Crucian Carp

Crucian carp are not an important anglers' fish, though they give good sport of light tackle. They are not widely distributed, being found in the main only in East Anglia, parts of south-eastern England, and in the meres in Cheshire and Shropshire into which they have been introduced.

They are somewhat similar to common carp in shape and appearance but the anal fin is short and they have no barbels.

The British record crucian carp weighed 5 lb 11 oz 8 drams. This exceptional fish was taken from a Surrey lake in 1994. Any crucian carp of 1 lb or over is reckoned to be a good one.

Laying-on and legering with crust, paste, worm or maggot baits are accepted angling methods.

Rudd

Rudd are very like roach in appearance, but if you compare the two you will see that the dorsal fin of a rudd is set much further back (i.e., towards the tail) than is that of a roach. Whereas the roach has a receding underlip (indicating that it does most of its feeding on or near the bottom), the underlip of the rudd protrudes slightly. They can also be gold in colour.

In Great Britain they are far less widely distributed than roach, their main natural home being the slow rivers and broads of East Anglia. They have been introduced into many lakes, ponds, pits and canals all over the country, however. There are comparatively few roach in Ireland (and those the results of fairly recent introductions) but there are countless rudd. Confusion arises from the fact that throughout Ireland rudd are called roach.

Rudd differ in feeding habits from roach. They are sometimes caught in winter but do not appear to be enthusiastic winter feeders. Their time is high summer and their place the surface waters. There they take flies and larvae, and they can be caught by fishing a small red worm, a pea-sized piece of paste or a single maggot on a no. 14 hook only a foot or 18 in below a tiny float.

Figure 24   Making a wire trace. Pass an inch of the wire through the eye of the swivel, bend it back on itself and twist firmly together. Attach a treble hook at the other end in the same way.

A matchstick or a piece of twig is better than a float if you can cast it far enough.

Normally you will need to cast a fair distance because rudd like to feed on the edges of reed or weed beds well out from the shore. In canals they cannot get far from the banks and here you should take every possible advantage of cover and remain as still as possible.

On stormy days a bait suspended a few inches above the bottom may be successful.

The rudd record, a fish of 4½ lb, has stood for a long time – since 1933. The seasonal lists of notable fish do not record many rudd entries above 3 lb.

Grayling

Known as the lady of the stream, grayling are members of the salmon family that happen to spawn in spring with the coarse fish.

They are patchily distributed and are most often found in trout waters. Large numbers are removed from such waters every year and put into coarse fish rivers, not, perhaps, to the benefit of the coarse fish, and so their distribution tends to widen from year to year.

They live in shoals and usually lie near a gravelly bottom ready at any moment to rise to surface flies. A maggot or small worm sent down with the current on float tackle so that it fishes about a foot off the bottom is likely to account for one or two grayling before the shoal is disturbed. They are sporting fighters and well worth a trial if you find they live in the river you fish.

Pike

As their general appearance and formidable jaws suggest, pike are predators, and they are the largest of our native coarse fish. They are found in rivers and lakes all over England, Scotland and Ireland. It is probable that the great limestone loughs of Ireland contain the biggest pike, weighing 50 lb and more, but in many waters a fish of more than 8 lb is a rarity. The record is held by a fish weighing 46 lb 13 oz caught at Llandegfedd in 1992. To catch the big ones, specially powerful tackle is necessary, and for normal pike fishing a rod at least as strong as those sold under the description 'carp rods' is needed. If you know of water containing pike of around 6 lb you can, with care, fish these with a general purpose rod.

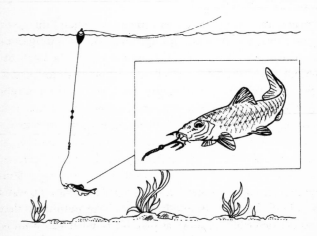

Figure 25   Float fishing for pike with a livebait. Detail: *liphooking the livebait.*

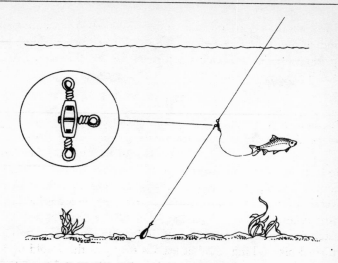

Figure 26   A paternoster tackle for pike: note that the livebait is hooked through the tail to reduce the risk of it swimming round the main line and causing a tangle. **Detail:** *3-way swivel, used in making up the tackle.*

Livebait Fishing

You may occasionally catch a very small pike when fishing with worms or maggots for other species, but if you are setting out to catch pike there is only one bait worth using – a small fish. Experienced pike anglers will tell you the best bait for pike is a live fish. The debate over livebaiting has raged on for a number of years, and many waters have banned the practice. The current record fish was caught on a lure. Plenty of big pike are taken on deadbaits, such as roach or rudd, but more popular nowadays are sea baits. Tackle shops sell frozen sprats, herring, smelt and others, but it is usually cheaper to go to a fishmonger. Some of the biggest pike are taken on half a mackerel from big waters such as Loch Lomond in Scotland. Avoid the monstrous floats sometimes described in shops as pike floats: what you want is a float just large enough, when cocked with two or three swan shots, to prevent your bait fish from pulling it under. Your line should never be lighter than 12 lb and you will need a *wire trace*

119

The correct way of unhooking pike. Slide the fingers in the slot under the jaw and draw the mouth open. Those sharp teeth are the reason for using forceps to remove the hooks – never use your fingers!

of about the same strength because a pike's teeth can easily bite through nylon. You can buy traces ready made up, but in the long run it is cheaper to buy a spool of single-strand wire from the tackle dealer, together with some size 8 treble hooks and swivels, and make up your own. Simply cut off a foot of wire with pliers and fasten a treble hook to one end and a swivel to the other (see *Figure 24*). After you have used it for some time, kinks may develop in your trace. Don't try to straighten these out, as the trace will permanently weakened. Throw it away and make a new one.

When tackling up, set the float so that the bait will be about 1½ feet above the bottom, pinch on the lowest split shot immediately above the trace and the others a foot higher up. Attach the bait by hooking one arm of the treble through its upper lip. Bleak, small roach, rudd, or any fish about 3 in long are all suitable baits for medium-sized pike.

Legering will account for big pike, and the methods are similar for other coarse fish, except the addition of a wire trace and fish for bait. Another method, which is excellent if you do not want to use livebaits, is wobbling. This involves mounting a deadbait on a treble hook rig, with nothing else on the line. Frozen fish are good as they are easier to keep on the hooks. If using fresh fish you can buy rig elastic from a tackle shop to keep it attached to the trace. The angler casts out the fish, lets it sink then retrieves it slowly for several turns of the handle. Let it sink again and just keep repeating the process. It is a good way of putting 'life' into a deadbait.

Where to Find Pike

Pike dislike fast water, and they like to strike at their prey from ambush. So you should look for them in slack water and laybys, in deep holes near swims frequented by smaller fish, and near reeds or other cover. When the river is swollen with rain water they tend to make their way into the backwaters. In lakes they can be harder to find, but again reedbeds, holes in the bottom and other natural cover are worth trying. Always cast a bait as gently as you can. A good point to remember is that because of the way a pike's eyes are set in its head, it is limited to what it can see below itself. This is worthy of note when thinking about bait presentation.

When to Strike

Pike can take baits at lightning speed, although they are also known to mess around with baits and turn them around. Whatever you have heard about striking with pike, remember, if in doubt strike straight away. As mentioned before, there is no excuse for the deep-hooking of pike, so never leave rods unattended, and keep your reactions fast. Although pike look fearsome they are one of the most delicate species, and you will do well to remember this when they are on the bank. Large landing nets are a must: 45 in is a good size.

Figure 27   Fishing a deadbait on the bottom. The root of the tail provides a secure anchorage for the hook.

Paternostering

A livebait can also be used on paternoster tackle. This is a useful method for fishing alongside a weedbed, since with ordinary float tackle it is difficult to prevent the livebait from swimming into the weed.

Spinning

Spinning consists of casting out an artificial lure, and reeling it back so as to make it imitate the behaviour of a live but injured fish. Special rods are made for spinning, but you can make do with your general purpose rod provided that you don't try to cast heavy weights. A good all round artificial spinner is a bar-spoon, about 1 in long. After casting, allow it to sink near to the bottom and reel it in fast enough to make the blade revolve round the central bar: study the action of the spinner in the water to judge the right speed, and vary it with occasional faster spurts. A natural fish bait can be retrieved more slowly, with occasional pauses to allow it to sink back towards the bottom. When a pike takes, strike at once.

Figure 28   A bar-spoon, one of the best artificial spinners: when it is drawn through the water the blade revolves around the mount, creating a flashing, fluttering effect.

Even small pike will take large baits, in this case a multi-hook lure.

Plugs are another lure to use and are becoming more and more popular. Used in America for years, and for many different species, they can be found in most tackle shops. There are even

Figure 29   A deadbait mounted for wobbling; various mounts can be bought ready-made, or you can make them up yourself.

mail order companies who specialise in importing these lures. Check the angling press for the appropriate adverts.

Unhooking a Pike

When you do land a pike, grip it across the back behind the gill covers and remove the hook with long-nosed pliers or artery forceps. The easiest way to unhook a pike is the following: lay the fish on its side and crouch over it with your legs either side to steady it. Slip a finger in the groove under its bottom jaw and gently open its mouth – the pike will have no other option but to oblige. Then remove the hooks with artery forceps (which you should never be without). Barbless hooks are the best type to use, but if you don't have any a good idea is to pinch the barbs flat on an ordinary hook with a pair of pliers. Do not put your bare fingers anywhere near the pike's mouth. Avoid the gills too, as they can cut you as well.

Never go pike fishing on your own if you don't feel confident – ask someone who's experienced to take you on a few trips. If you feel wary of unhooking, there is nothing wrong with wearing a glove.

Barbel

Barbel are a big species and very hard fighters. They would be high up on the fisherman's list if there were more of them, but they are limited to a few rivers.

They are found in the Thames, Kennet, Wiltshire and Hampshire Avons, Dorset Stour, in the Trent System, and in several rivers of the Yorkshire Plain. The latest run of big fish have come from the River Ouse in Bedfordshire. Stocks have been introduced with particular success into the Severn, and also into the Wye and the Medway.

They like deep pools, especially weir pools, in big rivers. Legering with lobworms or luncheon meat is the best method for them.

Catfish

The European catfish, or wels, has been introduced into still waters at Woburn, Claydon and Tring. They have also been stocked in several commercial fisheries at very big weights. A 99 lb specimen was taken in 1996, but it has not been established if this grew to that size here or was imported from abroad. These powerful and ugly fish grow extremely large and, like large eels, they are best fished for at night, using similar baits and techniques, but even stronger tackle. Large deadbaits produce results as do boilies, which are a high protein carp bait available from tackle shops. Alternatively, you can make them yourself, and any good carp fishing book will tell you how to do this.

Zander

These fiercely predatory fish look like — and in the past were often wrongly assumed to be — a cross between pike and perch. They are in fact a distinct species, and although not native to Britain, have been successfully introduced into parts of the Fens and Great Ouse system and into lakes at Woburn, Leighton Buzzard and Claydon. Fishing methods suitable for medium-sized pike will also catch zander (the record zander weighed 18 lb 10 oz).

Bleak, Gudgeon and Ruffe

Bleak are small silvery fish rarely exceeding 6 in in length. They swim in shoals in the surface waters of rivers with a slow or medium current.

Gudgeon live on gravelly river beds. They can be best caught on a very small worm or maggot trotted along the bottom on float tackle. Exceptionally they can weigh ¼ lb, but the average is 1½ to 2 ounces.

Ruffe (also ruff) are known as pope in some parts of the country. They are about 3 or 4 in long and look superficially like small perch, but they have no dark bars and the two dorsal fins are joined, not separate as in the perch. They are of no sporting interest except to match anglers.

A Final Word

I hope that when you read this page you will have read most of the book.

In your first season fish every sort of water you can find for as many species of fish as possible, using all the methods I have suggested. You will soon find what types of fish, water and methods please you most.

Remember to treat the fish you catch with the utmost care, and return them safely – who knows they might break a record another day!

Above all remember to enjoy your fishing and show consideration for other anglers on the bank. This is one of the friendliest sports in the world for young and old, with every angler sharing a common bond. Not just a desire to catch fish, but a love of nature and the outdoors – and this is worth preserving at all costs. Tight lines!

CHAPTER 8

Equipment Review

The world of fishing tackle is vast and can be a bit of a minefield as far as choice is concerned. These pages show a selection of tackle you will need straight away, and other more expensive items which can be bought further along in your angling career.

Rods

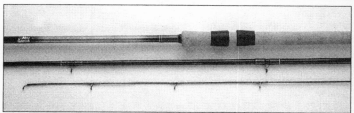

A typical float fishing rod is the ABU Gold Max Match.

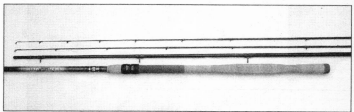

Another float rod is the Daiwa Matchwinner S.

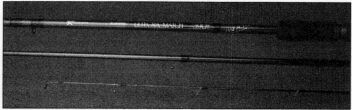

A serious match angler's tool: the Shimano Ultegra match rod.

127

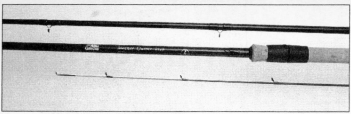

Legering needs a special rod. This ABU Maxxar Quivertip rod is more than adequate.

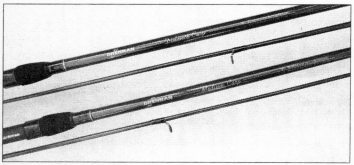

Big carp need stout rods to punch out baits and absorb powerful runs. These two, for medium and distance work, are made by Drennan.

Reels

This Silstar FRB 40 represents the budget end of coarse reels.

More money will get you a reel like this Shimano Super Match.

Closed-faced reels are perfect for trotting with a stick float. This model is made by Sundridge (left). Centre-pins can cost a great deal, but some anglers swear by them for trotting and close-in float fishing (right).

Poles

A good budget pole: the Shakespeare Onset.

More for the matchman: the Browning 7500 pole.

Seat Boxes

A Daiwa plastic seat box which is relatively cheap and ideal for the beginner (left). Watercraft make this mid-priced seat box, with several compartments for reels, floats and pole rigs (right).

This Team Daiwa seat box, with footrest attachment, is most likely to be used by match anglers and costs a considerable amount.

Holdalls

The ideal way to carry and store your rods is in a purpose made holdall like this. Nearly all tackle shops sell these.

Multi-purpose carryalls like this are a good way to carry bait boxes and accessories, including your keepnet.

Nets

Keepnets are available in various lengths and sizes of mesh (left). Here is a typical landing net for general fishing (right).

131

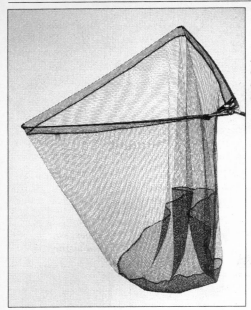

Bigger fish like pike and carp require a larger specimen net like this.

Accessories

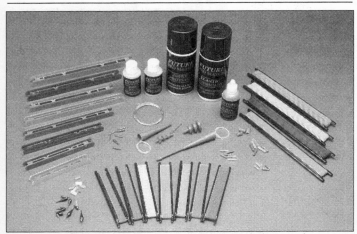

Pole specialists Future produce many accessories including winders, elastic, bungs, connectors and lubricants.

Rod rests are most important for comfortable static fishing. Shown here are types of floatfishing and legering (left). Catapults are excellent for accurate loosefeeding around your float. Larger types, with big rubber cups, are available for launching balls of groundbait great distances (right).

Winter fishing can be very uncomfortable. Thermal suits can be a great help in fighting off the cold (left).

Platforms are designed to give your seat box a level surface on angled banks. They can also be used for bait stands (below).

133

Lines

General types of fishing line made by Toray.

Drennan line for big fish (left). Braided line, such as this from Andico, is finding favour with lure anglers. With hardly any stretch, it gives a quicker response on the strike (right).

Hooks

Many different patterns of hook can be bought to suit various baits. These from Preston Innovations cater for offerings such as bread, maggot, bloodworm and squatts.

Hooks to nylon make life easier for those not proficient at tying spade-end hooks. Many companies make them, including these from Drennan.

Feeders

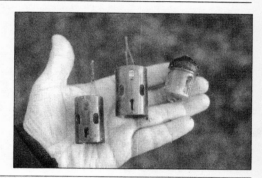

These are open-end swimfeeders for use with groundbait.

Blockend feeders are best for offering plenty of maggots.

Other Equipment

 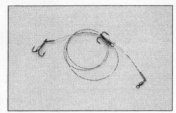

Plugs can be great takers of pike during the warmer months, but do occasionally account for fish in winter (left). A wire trace with treble hooks for pike fishing; known as a snap tackle. These can be bought ready made, or you can produce your own at home with separate items (right).

A set of scales takes the guesswork out of sizing fish. Most important if you catch a record specimen! (left)

Videos can be bought mail order from adverts in the angling press, or from tackle shops, and are a fun way of learning new skills (right).

Environment Agency Regional Offices

Anglian
Kingfisher House,
Goldhay Way, Orton Goldhay,
Peterborough, PE2 5ZR.
Telephone: 01733 371811

North West
Richard Fairclough House,
Knutsford Road,
Warrington, WA4 1HG.
Telephone: 01925 653999

Southern
Guildbourne House,
Chatsworth Road, Worthing,
West Sussex, BN11 1LD.
Telephone: 01903 832000

Thames
Kingsmeadow House,
Kingsmeadow Road,
Reading, Berkshire, RG1 8DQ.
Telephone: 01734 535000

North East
Rivers House,
21 Park Square South,
Leeds, LS1 2QG.
Telephone: 01132 440191

Midlands
Sapphire East,
550 Streetsbrook Road,
Solihull, B91 1QT.
Telephone: 0121 7112324

South West
Manley House,
Kestrel Way,
Exeter, EX2 7LQ.
Telephone: 01392 444000

Welsh
Rivers House/Plas-yr-afon,
St Mellons Business Park,
St Mellons, Cardiff, CF3 0LT.
Telephone: 01222 770088

EA POLLUTION HOTLINE: 0800 807060

Useful Contacts

**The Anglers Conservation
Association**
23 Castlegate, Grantham,
Lincs, NG31 6SW.
Telephone: 01476 561008

The Angling Times
Bretton Court, Bretton,
Peterborough,
Cambs, PE3 8DZ.
Telephone: 01733 266222

**British Record (rod–caught) Fish
Committee**
51A Queen Street, Newton Abbot,
Devon, TQ12 2QJ.
Telephone: 01626 331330

**The National Federation
of Anglers**
Halliday House, Eggington Junction,
Derbyshire, DE65 6GU.
Telephone: 01283 734735

Index

Page numbers in **bold** type refer to illustrations

Your Personal Fishing Record

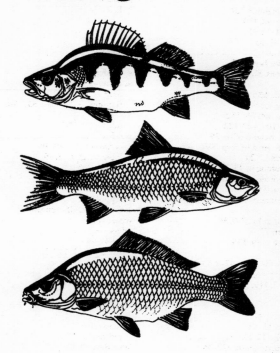

Date	Venue	Weather	Catch

Best Total Weight

Bait	Tackle	Comments

Date	Venue	Weather	Catch

Best Total Weight

Bait	Tackle	Comments

Date	Venue	Weather	Catch

Best Total Weight

Bait	Tackle	Comments